Cradle to Canoe

Camping and Canoeing with Children

ROLF AND DEBRA KRAIKER

The BOSTON
MILLS PRESS

Cataloguing in Publication Data

Kraiker, Rolf 1950-
Cradle to canoe: camping and canoeing with children

ISBN 1-55046-294-6

1. Canoe camping.
2. Family recreation.
I. Kraiker, Debra, 1960-
II. Title.

GV790.K72 1999   797.1'22'083   99-930277-9

03 02 01 00 99   1 2 3 4 5

Published in 1999 by
Boston Mills Press
132 Main Street
Erin, Ontario N0B 1T0
Tel 519-833-2407
Fax 519-833-2195
e-mail books@boston-mills.on.ca
www.boston-mills.on.ca

An affiliate of
Stoddart Publishing Co. Limited
34 Lesmill Road
Toronto, Ontario, Canada
M3B 2T6
Tel 416-445-3333
Fax 416-445-5967
e-mail gdsinc@genpub.com

Distributed in Canada by
General Distribution Services Limited
325 Humber College Boulevard
Toronto, Canada M9W 7C3
Orders 1-800-387-0141 Ontario & Quebec
Orders 1-800-387-0172 NW Ontario & Other Provinces
e-mail customer.service@ccmailgw.genpub.com
EDI Canadian Telebook S1150391

Distributed in the United States by
General Distribution Services Inc.
85 River Rock Drive, Suite 202
Buffalo, New York 14207-2170
Toll-free 1-800-805-1083
Toll-free fax 1-800-481-6207
e-mail gdsinc@genpub.com
www.genpub.com
PUBNET 6307949

All photographs by the authors

Cover design by Gillian Stead

Text design by Joseph Gisini / Page composition by Jonathan Freeman
Andrew Smith Graphics Inc.

Printed in Canada

Boston Mills Press gratefully acknowledges the Canada Council for the Arts, the Government of Canada through the Book Publishing Industry Development Program (BPIDP), and the Ontario Arts Council for their support of our publishing program.

To Grandpa, Willis Hawthorne

Listening to your childhood stories, like the times you struggled through waist-deep snow to get to school, nurtured the storyteller in all of us and inspired us to be adventurous.

Contents

It's hard to know when a child is ready to start wilderness travel, but ours benefited from starting young. By the time they were 7 and 10, they managed their own canoe and packs on trips.

Introduction

*I*N OUR QUEST TO SHARE THE WILDERNESS WE LOVE WITH OUR children, we encountered many challenges. We learned to adjust our expectations to accommodate their needs, and in return they have rewarded us with a new appreciation of the wilderness we love. By the time our boys reached the age of ten, they were already veterans of many wilderness canoe trips in remote destinations, from the sub-tropics to the arctic tundra. In the wilderness, we've found a bond that holds our family tightly together.

The canoe has always held a special fascination for us, and most summers find us spending every possible moment, from break-up to freeze-up, on the water. When we were married, we arrived at our wedding in a canoe, and our honeymoon was a canoe trip in northern Ontario. Our families learned to accept our passion for the wilderness, but when we announced to our parents that they were soon going to be grandparents, they naturally assumed that a baby would change our lifestyle and we'd settle down. We had other ideas.

"Surely you're not going to take the baby!" Grandma sputtered the first time we wanted to go on a trip.

The look on her face said it all: she didn't think a canoe trip was any place for us to be taking an infant, especially her grandson. Knowing Grandma, we expected this reaction (it seems to be in the job description) but what we didn't expect was a similar response from some of our long-time tripping friends. Any of our friends who had children, had waited until the children were "old enough" before taking them out. This magic age varied among the different families. Parents with more experience in traveling outdoors usually felt more comfortable taking their children into the wilderness at an earlier age.

Perhaps because of our many years of wilderness adventures, it never occurred to us that there might be an age when our children would be "too young" to come with us. We knew that having children would change the way in which we would experience the wilderness, but we were determined that having a baby wouldn't curtail our wilderness trips.

Not that long ago, North America was a vast, unspoiled wilderness, sparsely populated by small pockets of people, most of whom lived a nomadic life. Families moved with the seasons, traveling through the tractless landscape, following the migrating herds of animals upon which their lives depended for food and clothing. For countless generations, wilderness travel was as much a part of everyday life as breathing and eating.

When the Europeans came, they viewed the wilderness as a dangerous place that needed to be tamed before it was safe for civilized living. Eventually, gathering replaced hunting, agriculture and industry replaced the age of exploration, and the land was soon crisscrossed by a network of roads and rails. Wilderness travel was no longer necessary for the average citizen, and the skills to do it properly began to fall out of common knowledge.

In recent times there has been a strong interest in returning to the wilderness to provide a balance to our increasingly technological lives. There is no longer a *need* to go into the wild country, but many people now seek to challenge their skills in the wilderness and do so for what it can give them, not for what they can take from it.

For families, a wilderness trip can be an opportunity to slow down, enjoy life, and strengthen the bonds that hold them together.

In this book, we share the knowledge we've gained from many years of outdoor adventure in the company of our children. We hope it helps other parents acquire the confidence and knowledge to safely take their children into the wild.

Kids usually find lots of toys on their own when out on a camping trip, but it's a good idea to bring along one or two favorites from home.

Chapter 1

....

My How They Grow

TAKING CHILDREN ON CANOE TRIPS PRESENTS SOME UNIQUE opportunities and challenges. Children adapt well to canoeing and camping, but they need to be introduced to it gradually. The younger they are, the easier it is for the children to adapt, but the harder it is for parents to feel comfortable taking them into the wilderness. The hundreds of "what ifs" bombard us. What if they get fussy at night? What if they get sick? What if I can't handle it? What if we forget to take something?

Parents need to stage the introduction of outdoor adventure over several phases to ease the transition from the comforts of home to the more spartan living children will experience while camping. Regardless of the age of a child, begin his or her introduction close to home by going on easy outings to find out how your youngster will adapt to the outdoors.

As children grow during the years from infant to teenager, they pass through many milestones of mental and physical development. Each of these phases presents new challenges for parents to manage. As the child passes from crawling on all fours to their first tentative steps on wobbly legs, they are leaving behind a set of restrictions that confined them and are discovering a new freedom. When they learn to speak, they are soon able to express their feelings which helps them to explore the world in new ways. Through each of these changes, parents need to find the skills to nurture their children yet still protect them as their world expands. Taking them into the wilderness is an opportunity to broaden their horizons and build on the lessons they learn at home.

Canoeing and spending time with children in the natural environment has many rewards. Memories build, experience upon experience. Sitting at the water's edge, giggles and splashes as baby dips toes into the warm water. Teaching your little girl how to cast with her new fishing rod. Cuddling up in the hammock with a two-year-old, telling each other stories. Flipping through animal identification books with your pre-teen, trying to identify that brown, furry animal you just spent the last 15 minutes watching. Just having the opportunity to sit together by the campfire and watch the embers glow gives children and adults a time to enjoy each other's company. Peaceful days of summer become idyllic dreams to last a lifetime.

"When are children old enough to go camping and canoeing?" It is a common question that parents ask. There really isn't an age that is too young. If they can fit into a lifejacket, they can go canoeing!

Taking children into the wilderness isn't as difficult an undertaking as most people seem to think. The key is to start with simple, easy outings and build to more adventurous ones. An afternoon paddle is a great way to begin. You've got a whole lifetime together, so take your time and enjoy it; there's no need to rush into outings or attempt to accomplish too much all at once. Once your child is enjoying afternoon paddles, you can pack some meals and make a day of it. When the day trips become routine, start adventuring out on some overnight trips to established campgrounds. After camping out becomes a comfortable ritual, you can begin to travel to nearby wilderness destinations for overnight stays. Before you know it, you'll be able to spend as much time as you'd like in the outdoors.

While most children can be introduced to the outdoors at an early age, it is important that parents feel confident in taking their kids out. Parents need to have good canoeing and campsite skills for safety. If you're not sure of your skills, take some courses. They are readily available in most communities.

The canoe is a wonderful craft for family excursions. It is large enough to carry a considerable amount of gear and baby paraphernalia. The natural cradle-like rocking motion of the canoe easily lulls infants into a gentle sleep, which makes it easy to travel with young children.

Time spent growing up in a canoe helps infants and toddlers develop a heightened sense of the world around them. Most youngsters will sit and watch the world from a canoe as quietly as they will watch a cartoon on TV. It is natural for children to develop fears of the unknown, and at first they may not relish leaving the safety of home for a trip into the mysterious wilderness, but short adventures into local marshes to watch the birds and muskrats can help parents capitalize on their natural curiosity.

While a child's memory may not extend far into their past, it's hard to predict what events will be the ones that they remember. It's clear that, for our boys, some of the camping experiences in their early years had an influence on their lives. Even events now forgotten had a positive effect on them and made it easier to take them out as they got older. They may not remember details from trips made three or more years ago, but the way they currently feel about being outdoors has been an accumulation of all the years of experience they've had. Even as infants, they seemed to have carried enough memories through the winter so that they felt comfortable being outdoors as one-year-olds.

Getting Started

Children's needs are not that hard to meet in the outdoors. They need to feel safe, they need to be well fed, they need to be warm and dry, and they need to be entertained by what they're doing. When they're young, food is the main focus of their attention. As they grow older, food becomes less of a priority and entertainment becomes more important to them. Anticipating the children's needs as they grow makes it possible to introduce outdoor experiences during any stage of their development.

Babes in the Woods: The Feeding, Formula and Diapers Dilemma

What infants' needs lack in variety, they make up for in frequency. Infants are relatively easy to entertain, as their world doesn't extend much beyond the distance their arms can reach. As long as a familiar voice is nearby or they're being cuddled by someone they know, infants tend to be happy and content if they are well fed and dry. Taking care of a baby in the wilderness may be time-consuming, but it can be rewarding.

■ *Breastfeeding*

When taking an infant on a canoe or camping trip, two of the most difficult concerns are what to do about feeding and diapering. In this regard, breastfeeding mothers have it made. Probably the most difficult part will be finding a place away from bugs so both mother and baby can enjoy this quiet time.

A good solution is to create a shelter by using commercially available netting intended to cover a playpen. Any time that the baby is hungry and biting insects are a problem, it's just a matter of draping the cozy netting over mother's head and all around the baby. This doesn't take long to set up, and the peace and quite under the net make the effort worthwhile. Another option is to purchase a large piece of mosquito netting and either sew an elastic around the edges or put a casing (a tube of fabric) for a drawstring. Making one of your own means it can be whatever size you'd like. A piece of fabric 48 inches by 8 feet long will make a comfortable enclosed area if the material is folded in half on the long side and sewn together to make a bag about four feet wide and four feet deep. Folding the end over about an inch and sewing this in place creates a casing that allows a drawstring to be pulled through to close off the bottom. Once you're protected from the bugs, it's a wonderful feeling to lean back against a tree and breastfeed in comfort. The netting can be useful anytime you and your baby want to get out of the bugs, even if just to lie quietly in a hammock for a few minutes.

At home, breastfeeding mothers need to ensure that they eat well-balanced meals and drink plenty of fluids. This becomes even more critical when out canoeing. Because of the increased exposure to the sun and wind, as well as the higher levels of exercise, the fluid levels in their bodies will be depleted much more rapidly than they are accustomed to at home. It is important for both the mother's health and her ability to produce milk that she rehydrate by drinking fluids often.

■ *Bottle-feeding*

Babies that are on a formula diet are not quite as easy to care for, but they aren't much more fuss for parents. A baby's bottles can be sterilized for the next day while evening meals are being cooked. It's important to be sure that as much bacteria and contaminated matter has been eliminated from the water supply as possible. Use a filter pump to fill a pot

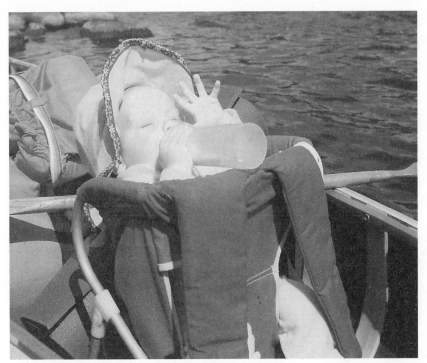

Bringing along some water that was sterilized in the morning means it doesn't take long to prepare a bottle when the baby gets hungry along the portage.

with clean water and put washed and rinsed nipples and rings in the water. Sterilize them by boiling them for several minutes. If this is being done over a fire, remember to cover the pot with a lid to keep ashes from getting into the pot. Check the level of water periodically; the last thing you want to do is to melt the nipples to the side of the pot.

Water for the baby's formula should also be drawn from a clean source by using a water filter pump. The filtered water should then be boiled for 5 to 7 minutes before using it to make up formula. Rather than dealing with the problems of carrying and sterilizing bottles, take along the bottle-shaped holders that use replaceable plastic liners. Once the water and the nipples are ready, simply pour the boiling water into the "bottle bags" and seal the contents with the nipples and lids.

Powdered formula is the only type that is practical and safe for camping. The powder will dissolve in water at room temperature. This means that the formula is basically only a scoop or two away from being ready at any time.

Never mix the baby's powder formula in advance. Mixed formula provides a rich medium for bacterial growth. The formula should only be added when the baby is ready for a bottle. Any leftover formula should be thrown out.

The early morning feeding is probably the most difficult. Our solution was to put a well-sealed baby bottle of sterilized water inside another waterproof container and put that into the bottom of one of our sleeping bags. This kept the bottle of sterile water at or near body temperature, which is exactly what the baby is expecting.

A critical element in preventing problem encounters with animals is to make sure there are no food smells in or near the tent. Never store a bottle of prepared formula inside your sleeping bag. This is not only an invitation to bears or raccoons to drop in for a midnight drink, but it is also dangerous because without refrigeration it can lead to food poisoning. When the baby is hungry, simply get the powder from the food pack, add it to the warm water and, *voila*, instant formula.

■ Baby foods

Pablum baby cereal is a perfect food to take camping with infants. On short outings, have the dry Pablum measured out in meal-size portions that can be carried in resealable plastic bags. Then it's simply a matter of adding sterilized water, mixing it up and serving it. For longer trips it may be just as convenient to bring the whole box instead of measuring out individual portions. The only drawback with this is in trying to keep the bowls in which to serve the Pablum sterile. If the thought of bringing all those little Ziplock bags is troubling, you might consider using a little plastic bowl with a tight-fitting lid. When the dishes are being washed and the baby bottle nipples are being sterilizing, boil the plastic bowl and lid too. Keep the sterilized bowl sealed until it's time to feed the infant.

It's good practice to sterilize some extra bottles of water the night before to keep on hand for the next day. When it comes time to prepare a meal of Pablum, there is no fuss, just open the bottle and stir.

■ Solid foods

Once a baby is comfortable eating cereals, the next food to be introduced into their diet should be vegetables. Vegetables are served before fruit because the infant will generally like the taste of the natural sugars in the fruits, so it may be hard to convince them to like vegetables after they've had fruit.

There are several options available for parents when the infant is being introduced to pureed fruits and vegetables. Bottled foods are one option, but glass jars may be as heavy as the food they contain, and there are places where bans on bottles and cans are in effect. Another concern when carrying bottled foods is the fear of breakage. If a jar breaks, it creates two problems: no food for the infant and contamination of other foods from broken glass. Bottled foods should be packed in a separate plastic container and secured in place with padding made from cardboard, much as they would be packed when shipped to the store.

Another option is to bring along the fresh vegetables that your infant is being introduced to. Prepare them by cooking them and mashing them well with a fork. The vegetables may need to be cooked more thoroughly than you would normally like, but it makes it much easier for serving to your infant. Squashes, sweet potatoes, carrots and rutabagas all travel well, though they can be a bit on the bulky side. If the infant is temperamental when it comes to textures and finds the fork method too chunky, it might be a good idea to bring along a hand-operated grinding mill for the food. We found that with a bit of extra effort we were able to coax our kids to eat the slightly chunkier foods.

Potato flakes are readily available at any supermarket. Adding potatoes to a meal is easy. Simply prepare as indicated in the instructions on the package. They are also great for thickening any vegetables for the baby if too much water was used when the food was mashed. Don't use potato flakes on camping trips if the child hasn't already been introduced to potatoes at home. No new food should be introduced to a child in a wilderness setting; there is always a risk of an allergic reaction. Solids should be introduced to infants one at a time to allow the baby to become accustomed to each food. This also allows the parent time watch the infant in the safety of the home environment for signs of any allergic reactions to the new foods as they are introduced. A canoe trip is not a good time to be faced with an emergency response to an allergic reaction to a new food.

For trips with an infant that will last a couple of weeks or more, it would be a good idea to be sure that the baby is eating a good range of vegetables before heading out. Having some variety in the diet is important, two weeks of just peas and carrots would be enough to make anybody cranky.

There is nothing to worry about if a baby decides they don't like the vegetables or fruits that were brought for them. For most of their first year, babies get the majority of their nutrients from breast milk or from formula. Going out on a camping trip should be a time to relax and enjoy. Infants who decide they don't want to eat peas aren't a cause for worry as long as they continue to drink breast milk or formula. In this situation, a little extra cereal or Pablum may be all that's necessary help mother and baby sleep contented.

Fruits can be introduced after babies are comfortable with a broad range of vegetables. Due to the natural sugars in fruits, infants tend to require little coaxing to eat them. Bringing fruits on a trip is easy, but it takes a little more time at home to properly prepare them for your backpack.

Fruit leathers are easy to make and easy to transport. Although this process is easiest if you have a food dryer, fruit leathers can be made quite simply in your oven at home. The only equipment that you need is a blender or food processor, a non-stick baking sheet and an oven. A fruit leather is produced by pouring a paste of pureed fruit, with the excess water and juices removed, onto a baking sheet, then slowly heating it in your oven to allow the remaining moisture to evaporate.

A wide variety in fruits can be turned into convenient-to-carry leathers. Because the process of drying the fruit has removed the moisture content, these fruit leathers will store safely for several months when they're properly wrapped. To serve these fruits while camping, just add sterilized, filtered water, wait for the fruit to rehydrate, stir and serve. The fruit will usually reabsorb the water faster if the filtered water has been heated a little first, but cold water will work quite well for most fruits, it is just a little slower.

As the infants' appetite for variety in foods grows and their tolerance of solids is established, planning camping meals becomes easier. Using pastas or rice as the base for meals, foods can be combined to allow planning of adult meals around an infant's diet. Most meals can be cooked with a minimum of fuss in just one pot.

Generally there are a number of foods in an infant's diet that can fulfill the baby's requirement for protein. There is little nutritional need to have meat for children on camping trips. If you want to include some protein foods in the camping menu, select them as you would at home.

When cooking meals that will be shared with an infant, the spices and seasonings (including salt) should not be added until the baby's portion has been separated.

Whenever possible, any mealtime routines that are observed at home at feeding times should be replicated while out camping. This helps both parent and infant relax and may be all that's required to prevent the struggle that it sometimes takes to get youngsters to eat.

Parents need to remember that snacks are a big part of older infants' eating routine. Baby cookies, crackers, Cheerios, Zwieback (a small, hard, toasted bread), or bread sticks also tend to be portable snacks that are favorites at home and on camping trips. Dried fruits may be an option, but they have a lot of concentrated natural sugars which should probably be avoided until after the baby is more than a year old. An exception that we made to this rule was dried apples that we dried ourselves at home.

Pack snacks in a way that makes them easily accessible while you are canoeing. One word of caution: If you are feeding your infant in the canoe, make sure the child is sitting in front of and facing you. If the infant starts choking on the snack you need to be able to react immediately without fear of tipping the canoe.

■ *Carriers*

One piece of equipment that we found invaluable for canoe camping trips was the chest-mounted infant carrier. When our boys were quite young, carrying them in an infant carrier was soothing for them. Select one that has a quick-release mechanism to allow the baby to be unsnapped quickly. These carriers keep infants up high enough that they can watch the scenery or the motion of the paddles. When they're tired of looking around, they can simply fall asleep, comforted by the sound of Mom or Dad's heartbeat. Carrying children in a front pouch carrier may not be as comfortable for the parent. Paddling is a little more awkward, and the parent who is occupied with the youngster may not be able to contribute much to the distance traveled.

When they were too big for this front-style carrier and they had gained sufficient head and neck control, our boys graduated to a backpack-style carrier with a stand. This carrier made portaging much easier and safer than carrying the baby in our arms. The boys were quite content with the movement of the hiking, and the snug harness made them feel secure. This carrier also doubled as a high chair when placed on level ground at the campsite. We could feed the kids and still keep our hands free for other things. There is always the possibility that the carrier may tip, so it is important that it always be placed somewhere that is within easy reach on a level footing. Staying close to the baby will mean they are less likely to be fussing because they'll feel included in the activities. It's also important to check that there are no rocks on the ground that might hurt the infant if the carrier does tip accidentally.

■ Diapers

Food usually only remains in our bodies for about a day. As part of the natural process, what goes in must come out! Dealing with this natural process is one of the major concerns when taking babies into the woods. The dilemma of whether to use cloth diapers or disposable diapers becomes an issue. The length of the canoe or camping trip is usually the most important factor in determining which option is best. It is a manageable task to pack enough disposable diapers into a back-pack to last for a weekend. However, it is not possible to pack enough disposable diapers for a two-week trip.

Taking along disposable diapers creates another problem — how to dispose of them in the wilderness. Some parks and wilderness areas require that all garbage be packed out for disposal. This means that those wonderful, rich-smelling treasures from the baby need to be brought back to a garbage bin at the end of the trip. This is a manage-able task for a short outing or a weekend trip, but the heavy bag of wet diapers accumulated on a long trip may not be a pleasant package to portage day after day. In addition, each night, this foul-smelling bag of diapers would need to be hung away from the reach of critters that might like to explore the contents.

Another option to deal with soiled disposable diapers where fires are permitted may be to burn them instead of carrying them out. Although it may not be the most aesthetic sight to watch an unrolled diaper burn in the campfire, the paper products of the diaper and their contents will burn completely if the fire is hot enough. Burning plastic releases toxic fumes, so it's a good idea to remove the waterproof plastic coating of the diaper prior to burning. The outer waterproof shell doesn't take much space and can easily be rinsed off and packed out in the garbage.

Taking used diapers back into the bush and burying them is not a good option. Animals are often attracted to these smells and may dig them up, leaving pieces of the diaper to litter the forest floor. Certainly this is not a pleasant sight for other wilderness adventurers.

Cloth diapers offer parents a workable alternative for camping. Carrying enough cloth diapers for two weeks will take up about as much space as disposable diapers for 3 or 4 days. The cloth diapers simply get used, washed and reused. The original form of cloth diaper, a single sheet of thin flannelette that needs to be folded and pinned in place, is probably more suitable for camping than the padded pre folded and fitted form. The single sheet of cloth may not seem convenient, but it will wash and dry quickly compared to a padded multi-layer cloth diaper.

There are drawbacks to using the cloth diaper. They tend not to keep the infant as dry as the disposable variety. This means spending a little extra time at campsites to allow time for washing clothes and diapers. In addition, there is always the concern that a diaper may leak overnight and dampen the sleeping bag. (Having to deal with a wet sleeping bag on camping trip is a problem that should be avoided.)

Doing the diaper laundry in the bush is relatively simple, but it is important to keep in mind that laundry water must be disposed of well away from the river or lake. One way to accomplish this is to take along a small plastic washtub. This tub should be light and fit nicely into one of the packs. The washtub creates a handy place for soaking and washing diapers, sleepers and infant clothes in a spot well away from environmentally sensitive areas. When the laundry is finished, it's a simple matter to carry the rinse water back into the bush and pour it into a hole dug into the active humus layer of soil. Use a non-phosphate, biodegradable soap. This washtub can also double as a "baby tub" for bathing before bed.

Extra diaper pins or safety pins provide a secure method of pinning the diapers to the line so they won't blow off and get dirty.

Extra diaper pins take a lot less space on a camping trip than clothes pegs do. Unfortunately, we can't always count on sunshine. There may be days when wet diapers may need to be hung under a tarp near the fire to dry. Another option is to drape them from a mesh drying net that is often found at the top of many good tents. It's a good idea to have a back-up plan and pack along a few extra sleepers and diapers than what should be required.

When our boys were infants, we always brought along a combination of both cloth and disposable diapers. We'd always use the disposable diapers overnight while the kids were sleeping, to make sure their sleeping bags didn't get wet. During the day we used cloth diapers. We tried to wash the sleepers and diapers as soon as we reached our campsite to give them time to dry before we went to bed. If they didn't get dry overnight, we would usually pin them on the top of one of the packs in the canoe when we started paddling in the morning, so the sun and wind would dry them.

■ *Canoe playpens*

We found that the canoe makes a wonderful playpen for infants when out camping. Bring the canoe up from the water's edge and set it up near the tents or kitchen area, where most of the activity is taking place. Find a level spot and secure the canoe so that is does not rock. A little rocking may be desirable, but only if the baby seems to enjoy it. A couple of rocks or small logs placed under either side of the canoe will help to accomplish this. Using the canoe as a playpen keeps the infant out of any wind and they are in a relatively clean environment.

Young babies seem to enjoy crawling around on the bottom and usually have no problem scrambling under the seats. Leaving some favorite toys in the canoe makes it more entertaining for them. Older infants may begin to pull themselves up using the seats or thwarts so they can see over the sides of the canoe if it's low enough. Usually the sides of the canoe are high enough that the baby can't get out but can see over and watch what's going on. As with any playpen, the baby still needs constant supervision and needs to be talked to.

Gently bouncing and swinging are other activities that tend to help an infant feel content. Most baby swings are too cumbersome to bring along in the canoe for camping trips. However, we found that with a little modification we could bring the major seat parts of either a small infant swing or a Jolly Jumper. We would securely tie the swing or the Jolly Jumper to healthy tree branch large enough to support the child's weight. To prevent problems with leg muscle development, it is important to set any bouncing chair so that the infant's feet are flat on the ground and not on their toes. Putting a tarp under them and suspending a few toys in front of them will keep baby happy and clean while the tents are being set up or the meals are being prepared.

■ Sleeptime

When sleeping with an infant in a tent, parents tend to worry about three things: making sure the baby stays warm, making sure the baby won't suffocate, and making sure they don't roll over on top of the baby. We used our packs inside the tent to create barriers that kept the baby from rolling far and also kept us from getting too close to the baby. Keeping the baby in a bunting bag and a child-size sleeping bag is important in order to prevent cold air from circulating around the baby. For our boys we made a polar fleece bunting bag. When the nights got colder, we combined the bunting bag with a sleeping bag. Inspect any bags or sleepers that are used for infants to ensure there are no loose cords that they can get tangled in.

Parents will have a preference for putting babies to sleep either on their sides, tummies or backs. If your child is a tummy sleeper, the puffiness of a sleeping bag may be a concern. Too much puffy material under a sleeping baby could cover their nose and interfere with their breathing. An extra piece of an insulated sleeping pad or an extra Thermarest mattress can be used inside the sleeping bag to provide a warm but harder surface for the baby to sleep on. A proper sleeping pad under this sleeping bag is important to keep the baby from being chilled by the cool ground. Air mattresses are not a good idea. These allow too much exchange of warm and cool air and will result in a cold surface beneath the sleeping infant. If the sleeping bag is too large, tie off the excess at the bottom so the baby can't crawl down into the bottom of the bag overnight.

Infants generally acquire a number of their primary (baby) teeth during their first year. During this time, they will chew on anything they can find. Take along a "chew toy." Put the chew toy in a water-proof bag and submerse it in the river or lake to cool it off. This should help soothe the baby's gums. Keep a small container of filtered or sterilized water nearby to rinse off the chew toy if it gets dirty. Rinsing a toy in the lake may not be a good idea, because even crystal-clear water can contain Giardia (beaver fever). Tying the toy on a short ribbon to the infant's clothing will help to keep it clean and within the baby's reach.

Very young infants will not want to lie down on the bottom of the canoe or be in a pouch carrier for an entire outing. Even though their eyesight is limited, they still like to see what is happening around them. A lightweight infant car seat with a carrying handle is ideal in the canoe and can be a safe sleeping area. While the baby is in the canoe they will have their personal floatation device (PFD) on and should not be strapped to the seat. In case the canoe accidentally tips, the baby's PFD should float them on the surface. Babies should wear a PFD whenever they're in a canoe or near the water, except in controlled situations such as a shallow beach for some supervised splashing fun.

In practice, it's actually easier to take an infant outdoors than it is an older child. Babies don't seem to mind at all. The timing of when parents start taking their kids on camping trips is usually more about how the parents feel about it than when children are able to go. The earlier that children begin, the easier it is to keep them going.

Tripping with Toddlers

Active toddlers are at the stage of development in which the world is an exciting place to explore. We can't kid-proof the wilderness, but when we take toddlers into the wilderness we need to educate them to "look, don't touch." We found that a toy camera helped to rein-force a "look, don't touch" game. We made sure the boys had their own toy cameras, and any time we got out of the canoe we put our cameras around our necks and the boys would copy us. We would look at lots of plants and pretend to take pictures, and they'd be busy shooting, too. In this way we were modeling the fact that wild plants should not be touched and should be left where they are, not put into their mouths.

As the toddler gets more mobile the canoe playpen becomes less effective. At this new stage, we would take a long, thin rope, and with our youngster's help we would mark out a big ring around the camp area. This would help the kids figure out where "my place" is and not wander into the "animals' place." Inside the rope boundary, the canoe playpen would be set on a large tarp. This way the toddler would remain relatively clean and would have their own play area. The few toys we brought along would be put into the canoe playpen to encourage the kids to stay in this area.

Leaving the toddler's lifejacket on while they are playing around the campsite provides an extra level of protection from falls. It is also somewhat reassuring to know that if a child does wander toward the water they have their lifejacket on. It also helps them to learn to automatically put their PFDs on. Keeping lifejackets on children helps them get accustomed to wearing them all the time you are camping.

For both adults and children, wearing a lifejacket on hot, humid days requires extra precautions. The lifejacket provides excellent insulation when the days are cool, but during hot spells, the insulation traps heat against the skin and prevents evaporation that would normally help to cool the body off. This can become a life-threatening situation if left unchecked. It's important to monitor the child's temperature and avoid this problem by letting them swim for a bit or by dipping the toddler's shirt into the water, then putting it back on under the life-jacket. This will help the child cool down.

A toddler will naturally want to move around in the canoe. Leaving a space in front of and immediately behind the bow (front) paddler free of packs gives the toddler space to move. It's easier to do this in the bow of the canoe, but the space could be made available in the stern, as long as there's no hurry to reach a destination. If the bow paddler is occupied with the toddler, the stern paddler may end up paddling solo a great deal. If the child is in the back of the canoe, the bow paddler can't keep the canoe traveling along, so the canoe just drifts until the child's needs are taken care of. It's hard to cover long distances when traveling with toddlers, so trips that have lots of options for campsites should be planned for kids of this age.

Having a toddler-sized paddle was important for our boys. Some of the time they would sit beside the canoeist in the bow, paddling along; other times they would lean over the gunwales just floating the paddle. It doesn't take too long for a toddler to realize that if they let go of the paddle it floats behind. They soon discover that it's a great

Children often develop irrational fears that are hard to calm. Camping trips can provide an opportunity for parents to help their children get over problems like being afraid of the dark or fearing animals.

game to let go of the paddle so that the parents have to go back to pick it up. The easiest solution for this is to tie one end of a string to the paddle's handle and the other end to the gunwales of the canoe. When the child releases the paddle, they can tow it back in again without help from the parents.

Having the child leaning over the gunwales makes some parents anxious. The child's lifejacket is designed to help them float with their head above the water. Both parent and child need to feel comfortable that the lifejacket will safely support the toddler in the water. Parents can understand that PFDs will keep the child safe, but children need to experience it before they will trust their lifejacket. Getting comfortable with the lifejacket is not something that should be left until the first canoe trip. This is best done in a heated community pool where the family can go and have a fun afternoon playing in the water. Toddlers may develop an irrational fear of water quite suddenly. The more opportunities they have to play in the water while wearing their

PFDs, the more comfort they'll have and the less likely it is that they'll suddenly become afraid.

Another thing that may increase a parent's level of comfort with toddlers who like to lean over the gunwales is a kind of toddler safety harness. Tie a rope from the toddler's lifejacket to your own. If they manage to fall into the drink, it doesn't take long to haul them back in by pulling on the rope.

Other than a paddle for the toddler, parents really don't need to bring along many toys. Children usually manage to make a lot of their own toys out of pieces of stick or small stones along the water's edge. Often kids find these toys preferable to the commercial toys that have come along on the trip. The one toy that we did bring that our boys liked to play with quite a bit was a small boat that was tied to a string. We called it the Boat on a Rope. When we were paddling in the canoe, the loose end of the string was tied to the gunwales or loosely to the child's wrist. They had lots of fun watching the waves created when they dragged the boat in the water or when they let the boat go and pulled it back in again. On shore they'd play with the boat along the water's edge. Having the string attached to the toddlers wrist meant that it could never float out too far and the child knew that they wouldn't loose it. Of course any time a child is near the water they should have adult supervision.

With all the fresh air and outdoor activity, children need their naps. Fortunately, toddlers tend to sleep well on the move. They just need a space to curl up. Keeping the space in front of the bow paddler free for this purpose is a good idea. The more confined space tends to help the child feel a little more secure and the bow paddler can keep an eye on them. The collar on the child's lifejacket acts like a little pillow but more padding may be helpful.

A collapsible umbrella is important to carry on any canoe trips with children. It is useful to provide shade for the child while napping in the canoe or onshore. It is also helpful in providing extra rain protection for the toddler in the canoe. Makes a special tent for the child in the bow of the canoe under their umbrella. When selecting an umbrella ensure that the points are well covered. Having the child help to pick it out in the store may also help the child enjoy napping and "hiding" under it.

■ *Feeding your toddler*

When the family's canoe trip menu is being planned, it's important to incorporate snacks, as they are essential for the toddler's health. With such small stomachs, toddlers need to eat more frequently. These meals can take on the form of healthy snacks that combine two or more of the food groups. During meals and snacks, toddlers will usually want to feed themselves, as they are at a stage when they are developing their newfound independence. This often means that more food goes on the ground than goes in their mouths. Pack a small vinyl tablecloth or a small nylon tarp to be used for mealtimes. Laying the tarp down on a flat area near you and putting the toddler's plate in the center of the tarp gives them a nice clean place to eat. Any food that does fall will land on the tarp, where it is okay for them to pick up and eat. As well, this "picnic blanket" prevents food from being scattered all over the camp area, where the scraps might attract critters looking for leftovers after dark. The tarp can also be used when toddlers are eating snacks in the canoe. It's easier to clean the tarp than it is to clean the canoe.

As long as children are not allergic to nuts, snack planning is relatively easy. GORP is a popular camping snack. GORP originally stood for Good Old Raisin and Peanuts, but the mixture has progressed beyond just raisins and peanuts. Nuts and seeds such as sunflower seeds are a good source of protein and are relatively high in fats, two nutrients that are important to a toddler's health. Both nuts and seeds are cholesterol-free. Fat that originates from plant sources does not contain cholesterol. Raisins or other dried fruits have natural sugars as well as assorted vitamins and minerals. It's hard to maintain good dental habits on camping trips, so it's a good idea to select dried fruits that are not too sticky. Dried apple chunks, small apricot chunks, unsalted pretzels and peanuts are among our favorite GORP components. Throwing a few chocolate chips or Smarties into the GORP mix makes a pleasant surprise.

For weekend outings, vegetables can be sliced into sticks and put in waterproof plastic bags that can be re-sealed. If there's room, bringing along a small freezer ice packs will keep the vegetables crisper longer. This is a healthy snack on its own, but serving raw vegetables with crackers and peanut butter makes an almost complete meal for a toddler.

One fruit that travels well and lasts many days on canoe trips is oranges. Half an orange combined with some Zwieback and cheese makes a healthy snack for your child.

Cheese is fairly easy to pack, but other sources of milk products may be a little more difficult. Milk powder is available in many forms. Whole milk powder is the best option, but it's hard to find. Skim milk powder is not as good for a toddler, but acceptable if whole milk powder is not available. Children need the extra fat content that whole milk provides for energy and growth. Milk powder is not always appealing to youngsters, so finding ways to disguise it may be necessary. Bringing a little chocolate powder to add to the milk powder can make the drink more acceptable. Instant puddings top the list of our favorite ways to hide milk powder. Adding a little more milk powder and water than the instant pudding mix directions call for makes something almost like a pudding milkshake. Adding milk powder to hot cereals just before serving them tends to hide the taste of the milk powder and adds the nutritional benefits of milk to the cereal.

Powdered juice crystals may be all right as a fluid replacement for the older crowd, but for the toddler, taking along a few juice boxes is probably worth the weight because of the added nutrition. When shopping for juice boxes to bring along, keep in mind that you want fruit juice not fruit drink or punch. Fruit drinks contain sugar, flavoring, coloring and water. Drinks labeled juice are made from squeezed fruits. Reading the label to see if there is extra sugar added is a good idea, then you can determine if the sugar content is appropriate for your child. Products labeled punch can be a combination of juices and flavored sugar water. Most drinking boxes generally have additional vitamin C added. Have a juice drinking box and snacks available for the end of a portage.

■ *Portaging*
Portages are a challenge for parents with toddlers. Toddlers tend to be a little too heavy to carry for long distances, yet they are a little too small to walk long distances over the portage on their own. This is where a parent's singing talents tend to come in handy.

We found portages were slow when the boys were young. While one adult carried most of the gear over the portage, the other would carry a manageable pack and take the youngster by the hand, walking along the trail and singing as many kids' songs as they could remember. It helps to listen to tapes of popular children's performers on the drive at the start of the trip. Regular stops along the portage to look at plants and insects helped to make portages a learning adventure, too. Counting steps is another way to pass the time. Depending on the age of your toddler, simply repeating 1 through 10 over and over can keep the young portager going.

When the kids were two, they wanted to have a backpack of their own. Even if the backpack is empty or only has their toy in it, it is important to let them. Over time, as they gain strength and balance, they can carry their own sleeping bag or clothes. We found that if we helped the kids to find a walking stick at the beginning of a portage, it sometimes gave them the extra boost of confidence to tackle the portage. It made them feel like a grown-up and helped to encourage them. Keep in mind that portaging is a lot of work for small legs. A few Smarties can help replenish the child's energy level.

Games like "I Spy" and "Show Me a Color" were also helpful along the portage or while paddling in the canoe. A toy camera and toy binoculars were an important part of our paddling gear when our kids were this age. Stopping frequently for a little rest and a closer look at nature seemed to take the work out of the portage. Traveling at this slow pace makes any pack feel even heavier than it really is. Keep this in mind when selecting a pack. It is important for maintaining your comfort and a good mood along the trail. You may need to carry your toddler for part of the way, so this weight factor needs to be taken into consideration for the sake of safety.

A child's temper tantrum along the portage can be frustrating for the parents. When you are hot and tired, the last thing you want to deal with is a screaming toddler. They have a way of knowing when you are not up to the challenge and seem to choose this exact time to have a tantrum. Try to deal with tantrums on the trail in almost the same way as you would at home. Walking slowly ahead up the trail and ignoring the tantrum behavior tends to work well. The trick is to monitor their safety without making it appear that you're paying any attention to them. You can hear them loud and clear, so you know everything is okay and they are not hurt. Pretending to stop and admire plants as you'd been doing before the tantrum gives you an opportunity to sneak a peek in their direction without seeming to. Singing their favorite songs may be enough to break through the tantrum and the child will want to join in instead of continuing with the screaming. If the tantrum is not getting them any attention, they will look for another strategy to get your attention. When they decide to come along, give them lots of praise and try to accommodate their requests.

We found that making up new lyrics to familiar children's songs helped us in the canoe and on the portage. For example to the tune of "Row, Row, Row Your Boat," we sang, "Hike, hike, hike the path/ looking for some birds/ Soon we'll be at our canoe/ and paddling once again." The bonus to singing the portages away is that many of the songs are set at a good pace for walking.

■ *At camp*

Once you get to camp, involving the youngster in the activities to set up camp helps you to keep track of them and gives them the satisfaction of helping. While setting up the tent, the child could be in charge of handing out the tent pegs and the unrolling of the tent. It's good to have a routine for the children. This helps them understand what they should be doing and prevents them from trying to do things that might damage the equipment. If the equipment isn't handled in an established routine, it's also likely that things may get lost. Practicing setting up tents at home will help to define the routine for your child and gives you the opportunity to work out any kinks.

Probably the most dangerous time on a camping trip for toddlers is while hot meals are being prepared. Giving the child duties to help out with food preparation serves two functions; safety and satisfaction. Any time food requires mixing, have the tot help to stir or mix, even if it really doesn't need it. If a fire is being used for cooking, having the child hand little sticks as they are needed for the fire. This saves time and teaches the child that working with fires is a task for big people. Keeping a small bag of GORP around while the meal is being prepared can help to stave off some of the hunger and will help to avoid some of the pre-supper whininess that kids occasionally get.

Toilet training is one developmental milestone that parents look forward to their child achieving. Having no more diapers to carry along or to wash makes the trip so much easier. Once you have started toilet training at home with your child, you certainly do not want to change the routine while you are out camping. However, leaning over a log or squatting is not easy for a little one, especially when they are just getting started with toilet training. This practice is different enough from what you've been struggling to teach them at home that they may get confused.

Plastic toilet training seats that fit on top of regular toilet seats are available at a reasonable cost. These seats are made of light plastic, so they do not weigh much, but they are sturdy enough to easily support the weight of the toddler. Suspending a couple of tree branches between two rocks, then setting the plastic seat on top provides the toddler with a comfortable toilet that looks close enough to what they're getting used to at home. In most provincial, state and national parks there are privies or box toilets. The plastic seat often fits nicely on these too. Once the toddler has control of their bladder and bowel movements, they may be introduced to methods to improvise a toilet seat in the bush, and the plastic seat can stay at home.

Whenever possible, routines that are being taught at home should be continued uninterrupted while out camping. Bedtime routines should match home routines. Brushing their teeth before bed is important for their dental health. Try to use as little toothpaste as possible when brushing their teeth and encourage them to spit out the excess, preferably somewhere where it won't be seen. Toothpaste will breakdown naturally, so spitting it out onto some small bushes is okay. If the tot has not yet mastered the art of spitting, try having a cup that they can dribble into. Rinsing their mouth out with filtered water is an important final step. Filtering the water for everything the child uses reduces the likelihood of water-borne illnesses. Don't rinse out toothbrushes in the river or lake; use the filtered water instead.

After they have snuggled into their sleeping bags and listened to a bedtime story, it is a good idea to pretend to lie down and sleep yourself. It is reassuring to them to know they are not alone in the big tent, listening to all the new sounds around them. We found that a candle lantern suspended from the tent ceiling was comforting. It also takes some of the damp chill out of the tent. When your toddler is finally asleep it is fine to slip out and join the other adults, but check on them occasionally and listen to make sure the child doesn't happen to wake up. If they do wake up, go to them right away to reassure them that you are there.

■ *Toys and tricks*
Most kids seem to think they'll need just about everything in their toy chest when they leave home on a camping trip. Anytime we give

toddlers choices, we need to ask questions in a way that allows us to live with their choices. "Would you like your yellow magic binoculars or your blue camera?" Either of these toys would be good to have along on a camping trip. The child will feel good that they were able to pick what they brought along and the parent will be comfortable with their child's choice. We encouraged our boys to take three toys with them when they were toddlers: a camera, a pair of binoculars and a boat on a string. These would go into their little backpacks. If your child can't sleep without a special toy, then you probably won't get much rest unless you bring that toy along. We tried to keep rotating bedtime toys at home so they didn't get attached to one particular toy. If the boys insisted on bringing a "snuggly" toy, we tried to have them pick one of the smallest ones we could manage. As a parental safety device, we used to pack a small favorite toy, but keep it hidden. If things got overwhelming for the toddler, we could haul out the toy as a surprise. We never had to use the hidden toy trick, but it might be a lifesaver for other parents.

To get your toddler used to sleeping in a tent, try sleeping as a family in the back yard. If there's room, pitch the tent in the middle of the living room and spend a night camped out there. This is a fun family adventure anyway! Role playing activities at home are a great way to encourage children. We had little tents that fit over the boy's beds and they loved pretending to be camping. They had toy canoes to be paddled in the bathtub and portaged cardboard boxes around the house. Any activities that simulated camping experiences were encouraged, as we wanted them to love camping as much as we do.

In order to get a toddler sitting rather than leaning over the side all the time, try bringing along a small stool. We used a plastic single step footstool. Two of these fit neatly across many canoes which makes a seating arrangement wide enough for three little ones to sit on. These plastic stools are also useful at the campsite as special chairs for the kids. They're not practical for long trips, but they're a great addition to include on weekend jaunts.

As a toddler grows and becomes a preschooler, patterns and routines usually become more important to them. They help to give the child a sense of control. Whatever morning routines your child has, allow them the time to go through them on canoeing trips. A bad start to the day will usually spill over into the rest of the day. If there is a home routine that simply cannot be duplicated in a tent or on a canoe trip, then try slowly changing it before you go camping.

Children's bedrooms can be decorated with outdoor themes to help them feel more comfortable. We found some glow-in-the-dark stars to put on their ceilings. We created a random pattern, but also made sure there was a distinguishable Big Dipper that was properly oriented and pointing to a North Star. If the kids were still awake when it was dark while we were out camping, we'd lay on our backs and look at the sky to locate the real Big Dipper. This gave the kids a good feeling and tied the outdoors nicely together with home. On a clear, bug-free night, it's worth waking the children up to take advantage of the opportunity.

At the preschool-age, children have vivid imaginations that may lead to unreasonable fears that have never surfaced before. Without warning, your child may suddenly become afraid of the dark or not want to go to sleep alone because they are afraid of monsters. Between the ages of three and four it may be difficult for children to distinguish between fantasy and reality. As a result, these new fears should not be taken lightly. When the child is tucked into their sleeping bag and doesn't want you to leave because a monster or a bear might get them, gentle reassurance and staying with them until they fall asleep are important.

The goal of taking children into the outdoors is to help them to appreciate nature and learn more about the environment around them, not to frighten them. This may mean less time sitting around the fire at night in the company of your friends, but spending the time with the child will pay dividends in the morning. A well-rested child is usually a lot happier, and the overall experience will be more positive for them.

At three or four years of age, children lose some of their body fat and their faces tend to take on more mature characteristics. They are physically stronger and should be encouraged to carry a little more weight in their backpacks. A sleeping bag is a good choice, because it is usually fairly bulky but not heavy. In a child-sized backpack it looks like they are carrying a lot and this seems to give most preschoolers a strong sense of pride that they can carry such a big load. As with a child of any age, give lots of praise and encouragement. A hug goes a long way when your child has carried their pack over the entire portage.

Growing Nature Nuts

Canoeing with a school-aged child can offer both parent and child a chance to sit quietly by the campfire and get to know each other better. The transition from baby to boy seemed to happen quickly with our children.

A school-age child is big enough that parents may want to consider options other than having a third paddler in the canoe. Of course, if the child wants to paddle in the bow while one of the adults gets to sit in the middle and relax, the opportunity is there. However, many families with school-age children are more likely to graduate to the next level and add a second canoe to the flotilla. Traveling with infants seems to require more gear than traveling with school-age children, but the trade off is by no means equal. The extra diapers and toys may take up more space, but they're still a lot lighter than another canoe.

Depending on the skill level of the parents and the number and ages of the children, there may be benefits in taking out two canoes with an adult in the stern of each. To accommodate a growing family, it may be necessary to take some canoeing courses and spend a bit of time looking for an appropriate second canoe. In our family, we began paddling in two canoes when our oldest son reached school-age. At this age children are developing confidence in their skills and beginning to be able to learn some of the paddling techniques. These will be fostered much faster from their new positions of responsibility than from just sitting in the middle of the canoe. It's important that the adults have refined their skills because until the child is strong enough to contribute, it is almost as though the adult is paddling solo.

The distribution of weight in a canoe is important to make the canoe handle properly. If the front is too light, it can be hard to paddle into even a light wind. One helpful hint when you have a small paddling partner is to rearrange the packs and perhaps even change the seating arrangements. This can be accomplished in a number of ways. As the child is much lighter, putting the heavy packs right up behind their seat tends to restore some of the balance. Small children don't need a lot of room, so it's usually possible to put a large, heavy pack in front of the child. Another method of adjusting the weight distribution is to move the adult closer to the center of the canoe. To accomplish this, simply spin the canoe around and paddle it backwards. This means the adult will sit on the wider bow seat facing the middle of the canoe and their little partner will sit on the narrower seat facing to stern of the canoe. Paddling the canoe backwards like this not only helps with the balance of the canoe but also puts the child in a narrow part of the canoe making it easier for them to reach the water with their paddle. This arrangement puts the adult into the solo canoe position that makes it easier to maneuver the canoe.

School-age children may still need to nap. The first clue that a nap may be required is a little grumpiness from the youngster. When your bow partner does nod off for a nap and stops contributing to the paddling, being closer to the center of the canoe will make paddling easier, especially if the route has some meandering streams.

After spending some time paddling in the bow, most children will eventually want to try to be responsible for steering the canoe and ask to paddle in the stern. It is opportunities like this when your child is willing and wants to learn that you can introduce some of the basic paddle strokes. You can anticipate a slow but scenic route as the canoe zigzags like the little doodlebugs that are often found on shallow water. As long as the child gets encouragement, it is a lot of fun. With some coaching and lots of practice, things will eventually straighten out.

When there is some leisure time at a campsite, older kids will often ask to go out to paddle the canoe by themselves. The danger with letting them do this is that they may not be able to get the canoe maneuvered back toward shore. Initially, we would only let the kids paddle the canoe in an enclosed area such as a small bay and they had to be accompanied by an adult. After a while we tried another solution. We simply tied a long rope from the bow of the canoe to a tree or some large rocks on shore. This way they could only go as far as the length of the rope. We'd only let them do this under our supervision and if they were having a hard time getting the canoe maneuvered back to shore it was a simple matter to grab the rope and pull them in. Paddling a "boat on a rope" was a lot of fun for the kids and they had an opportunity to practice their new strokes in safety.

If the children's enthusiasm is keen and their paddling abilities improve, it may be time to consider acquiring a kid-sized canoe. We found a light canoe for the kids to paddle. The kids would paddle their canoe filled with their packs while we used one of our adult-sized canoes. This was an ideal way to enjoy short, leisurely weekend trips. Paddling their own canoe develops a strong sense of independence and competence. Paddling at the kids' rate may be a little slow for some adults, but it is important for the children's self-esteem to have them keep up with or be slightly ahead of the adults. It is important for safety too; to keep the kids in sight and nearby at all times. This is almost like letting children cross at a crosswalk by themselves for the first time. Safety always comes first. If it becomes windy or the kids are experiencing difficulty maintaining their course, attaching a rope from the adult's canoe to the kid's canoe will help everyone to feel safer.

When a child enters school their horizon expands. They develop new friendships and their parents are no longer the center of their universe. Letting your youngster invite a friend to come along for the weekend canoe trip can be a lot of fun for your child. This gives your child a chance to show off their safe camp skills and teach these to one of their friends. This may mean the end of a quiet family weekend, but it helps to solidify the importance of canoeing and camping for your child. (It can also improve your child's social standing with their peers if their friends think it's cool.)

School-age kids like rules. It gives them a sense of security as well as something to complain about. When they are given the opportunity to be part of the rule-making team, these rules take on even more importance. Camping rules are almost always based on safety and include things like camp boundaries, fire safety and canoe safety.

About the same time your child graduates to paddling their own canoe, they may be graduating into their own tent, too. This is a big, frightening step for both parents and children. You might consider shopping for a tent together. Let them crawl inside and lie down and see how it feels. Tent quality is important; a tent that leaks in the middle of the night will not be pleasant experience.

To ease the transition, start by having the kids sleep together in a tent in the backyard in an environment they are comfortable in. Even if they only last one hour in their backyard campsite, praise their efforts. Even the familiar night sounds from around home seem close and ominous at night and the kids may be frightened from a tent of their own on their first night alone. Having their own flashlight with them is also important as this gives them a sense of control over the darkness and they'll know they can find the back door of the house with no problems.

When packing for the next weekend getaway, ask the children if they want to take their own tent. Chances are they will but they may decide against sleeping in it when night falls. Make sure the other tent you bring has enough room in it for everybody. Sometimes, even with all the groundwork done, Mother Nature plays a role in changing these plans.

When our boys were seven and ten years old, we spent the entire month of July on a canoe trip in Ontario to prepare for an arctic adventure we'd be doing the following year. Before going on the trip we'd prepared the boys and the two of them were keen to be sleeping in their own tent. Knowing that this might not last for the whole trip, we brought along the four-person tent we usually use, as well as their two-person tent. They were excited about being independent and had no problems setting up their own tent and got their sleeping pads and sleeping bags all set up before supper on our first night out. When night fell, armed with their own headlamps, they happily went off to their own tent and proceeded to talk and giggle for the next couple of hours. We were quite surprised to see that our youngest son Brendan was so content, as he was still afraid of the dark at home. Being with his big brother seemed to be all that he needed.

The second night began much as the first had. The boys organized their own tent and went readily to bed with little coaxing. They spent a similar amount of time giggling and carrying on, but after enough reminders they slipped quietly into sleep again. Some time in the middle of the night, a violent thunderstorm and torrential downpour hit the area where we were camping. It didn't take too many of the brilliant cracks of lightning and incredibly loud thunder before our two boys came racing into our tent for the rest of the night.

For the next two weeks any talk of setting up their own tent was met with a resounding "no way thank you." Near the end of the trip they started setting up their own tent again. Their only condition was that the door of the "kids tent" needed to be butted up next to one of big tent's doors. They knew that any time they wanted to, they could unzip their tent and crawl into ours. This was like having a two-room tent and gave them a feeling of confidence again. By the end of the trip, the "kids tent" could be pitched a little farther away, and they were once again talking and giggling for hours before they finally dozed off for the rest of the night.

Moving the children to their own tent may cause parental fears of "sleepwalking kids" wandering off into the wilderness. Zippers, regardless of what they are made of, are noisy. If you are worried that a sudden "zip" in the night won't wake you, tie a couple of bells to the zipper pull. Anytime the bells ring and there is a resounding "zip" in the night, you know one of the kids has escaped and you can talk to them or follow them out.

On some canoe trips you may decide to sleep one adult per tent with the kids. This can be helpful to the parent-child relationships. Sometimes with the hustle and bustle of everyday life we may not get enough time just to sit and talk with our children. Quiet time in a tent is a great opportunity to chat, and kids seem to really appreciate the chance to spend time with their parents.

The younger a child is when you start canoeing and camping with them, the more natural being in the outdoors is for the child. Rather than "How old should they be?" perhaps the question should be "How young can they be?" Canoeing and camping will become part of their lifestyle if they've done it so often that they rarely think twice about it. Parents taking children into the outdoors need to have realistic expectations and understand normal stages of development. Good food and adequate rest are essential. Setting trip goals that are attainable and schedules that are realistic for the children will help to keep everyone happy. A child's recollections of the days they spent canoeing and camping should be among the best of their lives.

Young bodies are more affected by the environment than adults' are.
It's hard to imagine how cold it might get on a trip while packing at home.
This is August 3 in the NWT.

Chapter 2

....

Clothing

WHILE AT HOME, THE TYPE OF CLOTHING WE WEAR AND THE WAY we dress isn't critical. If we get too hot or cold we simply go inside or change our clothes. When we go out into the wilderness, however, we're much more dependent on our clothing to provide us with protection from the elements. Many outdoor adventures result in unpleasant memories because clothing did not do its job. For some people, getting cold and wet may cause an aversion to camping that can last a lifetime. But the problem can be a lot more serious than that, it can go beyond mere inconvenience and become life-threatening. If inappropriate clothing permits the body's core temperature to fall too low or rise too high, all sorts of problems can occur. Understanding how clothing systems and fabrics function is fundamental to keeping family outings safe. As parents we are not only responsible for our own levels of comfort and warmth, but we must also help our children do the same.

The Layering System
Good outdoor clothing is based on a layering system. The various layers must work together to protect the body from the elements and to help the body maintain or dissipate the correct amount of heat to help you feel comfortable. Balancing these comfort factors means matching clothing to the body's level of activity within the environment.

Our bodies try to get rid of excess heat by perspiring. A good clothing system will allow this moisture to be moved away from the skin so it can evaporate naturally. If it remains in the fabric, the wetness becomes a conductive layer that will chill the body quickly.

Clothing systems usually involve a series of three layers: a wicking layer, an insulating layer, and a protective layer.

The wicking layer is the one that touches the skin. The fabric for this layer should not absorb moisture but should transfer the moisture through it, away from the body. This garment should be body-hugging but not restrictive.

The insulating layer helps the body maintain its warmth. Ideally, this fabric should allow moisture to transfer through the insulating layer yet provide pockets of air to trap warmth. The insulating layer can be made up of two or three loose-fitting items that will dry quickly and maintain their insulation value even when wet.

The outer layer is the protective layer, which should keep both the body and the underlying layers of clothing away from the elements.

The trick to keeping warm is to allow the moisture vapor generated by the body to escape through this protective layer, especially from the body's hot spots — the crotch, the underarm, the neck and upper back.

A complete clothing system also takes into consideration the type of protective wear on your feet, hands and head. Since we lose a great deal of heat from our extremities, keeping them covered up is vital in cool weather. During moderate activity our hands sweat. If that moisture remains in our mitts, our hands will become cold. Our feet sweat, too, perspiring more freely than almost any other part of the body. Active feet can sweat as much as one cup each per day. Your boots and socks need to be able to get rid this moisture. Wet feet are not only uncomfortable and cold, but they are also more prone to blisters and other foot ailments.

High heat areas
The head is a critical source of heat loss. The head has many blood vessels that supply the brain with food, oxygen and energy. If the head is uncovered at temperatures of 40 F (4 C), you can lose up to fifty percent of your body heat through the top of your head. As the temperature drops further, heat loss accelerates. At 5 F (-15 C) this

heat loss can be has high as seventy-five percent. Mom was right! Wearing a hat, which allows the moisture to move from the surface of your head without losing heat, is critical to cold weather comfort. In warm weather, taking advantage of this heat loss can make us much more comfortable. Wearing a dampened bandanna, a wet hat or wetting your hair can help to draw large amounts of heat away from your body and cool you off quickly.

Whether you are planning the clothing system for yourself or for your child, correctly selecting fabrics, fabric finishes and fabric laminates for your garments can greatly increase your ability to stay comfortable.

Selecting fabrics
The absorbency and comfort of cotton is familiar to every parent with an infant in cloth diapers. Fibers that can absorb moisture are termed hydrophilic ("water-loving"). All natural fibers, plus rayon and acetate, are hydrophilic. Because moisture is easily absorbed, these fabrics tend to dry slowly. They may also shrink or lose shape. Since they absorb moisture easily and are slow to dry, hydrophilic fabrics may not only be uncomfortable but can also draw valuable heat from the body and accelerate heat loss. A wet, cold toddler is not a happy camper. Clothing systems for youngsters should not include much cotton or other natural fibers.

Wool is also a natural hydrophilic fiber. Wet wool sweaters and pants can become extremely heavy. Unlike other natural fibers, however, wool will help draw moisture away from the skin. Because wool is made from the hair of animals, the fibers in the fabric act just like our own hair. When there is a lot of humidity in the air, the natural curly hair becomes even curlier, producing trapped air pockets that allow the garment to maintain its insulation. Moisture passes into the garment increasing its weight.

Since the 1920s, science has been developing man-made fibers and experimenting with various methods of fabric construction. Unlike natural fibers, most of these man-made fibers are hydrophobic ("water fearing"). Fabrics made from these fibers will not absorb moisture.

Since the warmth and insulation values of wool can now be produced in hydrophobic materials, the benefits of outfitting a family in these synthetic fabrics are obvious.

Popular polyester "Polar" or "Arctic" fleece fabrics have revolution-ized the outdoor-garment industry. Fleece fabrics come in a wide range of qualities, from bargain store to haute couture. Lower-quality fleece fabrics tend to feel hard in your hand when you squeeze them and tend to pill (develop little balls of fiber on the surface) soon after the first wearing. Another way to measure the quality of the fleece is to hold the fabric up to a light. If you can see light through the fabric, you can be guaranteed that the wind will whip through the fabric, too. Good-quality fleece tends to be warmer and will look good for many years. Thrifty shoppers may find these higher quality items in second-hand shops.

Polar fleece is available in a variety of weights or thicknesses. Wearing layers of various thicknesses of fleece makes it easier to adjust the amount of insulation. This will let you adjust for temperature ranges. Because "polar fleece" is hydrophobic, it will not hold much moisture even if it becomes completely submersed in water. Squeezing out the water by hand and spinning it over your head will make the wet garment fairly comfortable to wear and help it maintain its insula-tion value.

Purchasing quality fleece garments for your family will be a good long-term investment in comfort and warmth. Avoid those items with cotton-knit cuffs and collars, as they retain moisture. A narrow elastic cuff in spandex is better. The textile fleece industry is constantly making advances in technology and knowledgeable salespeople at specialty retailers can provide a wealth of information.

Spandex (sometimes referred to by one of its brand names, Lycra) allows fabrics to stretch yet bounce back to their original shape. These garments cling to the body and tend to be less bulky under the arms and around joints such as the knees and elbows. This reduction in bulk is a big advantage to the younger generation of campers.

One of the lightest yet strongest man-made fibers is nylon. It is abrasion resistant, durable, does not deteriorate with age, and has been used in outdoor packs and tents for years. Nylon fabrics are available in various thicknesses, from heavy-duty Cordura, suitable for packs, to soft and delicate fabrics for undergarments. This makes it one of the most versatile fabrics. The whistle that comes from between the legs of youngsters walking in nylon-polyester snowsuits is one that is familiar to many parents. Some nylon can be quite stiff and noisy to wear, but

This campsite in Big Trout Lake in Algonquin sloped down to the water. We kept Kyle safe by attaching a line to his PFD and clipping it to a rope between two trees. If he tripped, the PFD protected him and the rope stopped a tumble.

nylon fabrics can be finished in such a manner that they look and feel like cotton.

They do not fade easily and mud and dirt do not penetrate the fibers of the nylon fabrics, which makes cleaning relatively easy. For these reasons, nylon has been used as the outside covering for lifejackets and backpacks for years. The various thicknesses of the nylon filaments can make a remarkable difference in the feel of the fabric. Microfibers are filaments that are so fine that they are thinner than the thread of the silkworm. Garments made from nylon microfibers can be water and wind resistant, breathable, strong and cottony soft.

Not only are nylon garments more durable, but they also reduce the need to bring several changes of clothing and they compress extremely well in a pack. Two complete changes of nylon pants and shirts take up as much space as one pair of cotton twill or wool pants.

Appropriate layers of polar fleece under a nylon outer shell should prove a good choice as a clothing system for children.

Outfitting Infants

Chances are you will try a few day trips first before attempting your first overnight adventure with an infant. Day trips sometimes can be more dangerous than overnighters, for the simple reason that we tend not to be as prepared for changes in weather. It may be wonderful and warm when you depart, but clouds may roll in and dramatically change the day. Young people tend to need more changes of clothing and more layers than do adults. Even with something as simple as a leaking diaper, the child will need a complete change of clothing, from base or underwear layer through insulating layer and possibly even a new protective layer.

Diaper shirts are used to help insulate an infant and draw moisture away. Most are made from cotton, but cotton-polyester blends are also available at department stores. Obviously the higher the polyester content, the less moisture it will absorb. Single-layer diaper shirts will dry relatively quickly, even with a little cotton content. Some parents may prefer to simply dress their babies in two layers of sleepers. Sleepers are available at department stores in 100-percent polyester and in cotton-polyester blends. The base layer, the sleeper closest to the baby's skin, should be relatively thin, and the weave of the fabric probably shouldn't be tight. This will allow moisture to pass through the base layer. Any time you select a natural-fiber blend, the clothing will absorb more moisture and take longer to dry.

For cold mornings, use one or more layers of various weights of good-quality polar fleece. Additionally an insulated bunting bag (like a sleeping bag with sleeves) will help the infant maintain warmth. When planning the fleece layering system, start with a fleece sleeper, then cover this with a long-sleeve fleece romper outfit and perhaps a pair of fleece overalls. As the day gets warmer, layers can be removed.

Selecting outfits with peek-a-boo cuffs for hands and feet will give parents the option of having the hands and feet free or covered. The type of protective layer worn over top of the insulation layer will depend on the weather. A wind-resistant nylon shell may be all that is required, or a waterproof shell may be necessary if rain threatens.

If the afternoon turns hot, remove the insulation layers and replace them with a layer that protects against the sun. This should be made from a thin, tightly woven fabric. Brushed-nylon microfiber fabrics are an ideal choice. Finding such outfits in infant sizes may be difficult. An alternative is a polyester-cotton bunting bag or long-sleeve romper suit in a light color that will reflect sun's rays. Children under the age of six months should not have sunblock creams applied to their skin. Instead, cover them with thin layer of protective clothing. Sun hats should be wide-brimmed and fitted with a chin-strap so that the child cannot easily remove it. An umbrella can a be used for additional shade.

If you are planning to stay out overnight, take several changes of clothes, especially the base and insulation layers. Think of the number of times a child's clothing is changed at home and add more.

■ Cold weather camping with infants

When camping in the spring or in late summer or fall, your infant's clothing system should include leggings and a coat with an attached hood. If your child isn't walking yet, a hooded bunting bag may be more appropriate. This layer doesn't have to be waterproof. The waterproof layer can be an additional layer on top. Warm hats, mitts and boots are essential. Some sleepers come with sewn-in feet. If these are made with polar fleece, they will be warm. If the infant is not yet walking, covering the child's feet with extra polar fleece socks may be all that's required. Once the child becomes mobile, they'll need boots that are big enough to slide over the feet of their sleepers.

When parents are paddling, they're generating heat and keeping warm through exercise. Because infants are not participating in this activity, they may need to be bundled up more. Dress them warmly and keep them out of the wind.

Our boys hardly ever managed to remain completely in their sleeping bags at night. Because they spent so much time outside their sleeping bags, warm polar fleece "pajamas" were the sleeper of choice for us. Using a polar fleece liner inside the sleeping bag may be an option to consider. This tends to roll with the body and therefore keep the child a little warmer overnight.

Toddler clothes

As the child gets older, sleepers should still be used at night, but daytime clothing will change slightly. They can now wear polar fleece and long-sleeve polyester rompers or tracksuits. The romper suits or tracksuits should be covered with a nylon warm-up suit, which will keep the romper cleaner and prevent the wind from robbing the child of heat. Additionally, if the nylon is woven tightly enough it will help to prevent bugs from biting though the layers of clothing.

For warmer days, relatively thin long-sleeve T-shirts that contain at least sixty-five-percent polyester are available in department stores. While a toddler can wear sunblock, protecting their skin further with light-colored clothing is a good idea. Wide-brimmed hats are always a good choice for sun protection, regardless of the person's age. Eye protection is important, as well. If you can convince your tot to leave sunglasses on, then getting them a pair is probably a good idea.

When the child is being potty trained, changing to two-piece outfits makes it easier for them to be independent. The trade-off is that their shirts may ride up and expose their backs or tummies, exposing skin to bugs. Blackflies are the worst because they'll often go inside small gaps in clothing and settle in for a meal. One summer weekend when Brendan was still little, we wanted to give him a little independence. Though we did our best, constantly pulling down and tucking in his T-shirt. The blackflies still managed to find exposed skin. The next weekend we changed tactics. We took a couple of pairs of his overalls with the Velcro tabs at the shoulders and sewed one of the shoulders shut. On the shoulder that could be opened, we sewed a big button so that he could remember which side to undo. He could get the pants undone by himself when he needed to go to the washroom and he could get himself dressed again, except for the one side that had to be closed with the Velcro tab. Even if the other side didn't get done up, his pants would stay up and the blackflies couldn't get to him as easily.

■ *Footwear for toddlers and preschoolers*

Once children become mobile, appropriate footwear becomes an issue. It's important to keep their feet dry, warm and protected. During the summer, we brought rubber boots and two pairs of running shoes for each of our boys. One pair of running shoes was designated "wet shoes" and could be worn in the water. Wet shoes should have mesh panels or drain holes to let the water drain out quickly. Shoes are now being manufactured that are designed to be worn in the water. A well-made sport sandal is also a good option, as these may not come off as easily while running around in the water and will dry much quicker than traditional running shoes. It is important to wear footwear in the water to avoid injury. Even when you find a nice, safe beach, it's still possible that there might be something under the water that could cut their feet, such as clamshells. Why take the chance? The second pair of running shoes were kept as "dry shoes" and were only worn around camp and on days when portages seemed dry.

We dressed our kids in rubber boots when the days were wet. Two layers of socks are necessary to keep feet dry. Put "liner socks" that are not cotton on their feet and follow these with a second pair that are a little thicker. Sock layering should keep the feet dryer and free from blisters.

■ As their feet get bigger

Shoe and boot requirements for older children are similar to those for adults. The type of trip you are taking will determine whether hiking boots will be necessary. If portages are more challenging, then you may opt for a hiking boot. Also if you plan to set up camp and stay for a few days and go for some day hikes, then hikers for everyone may be warranted.

The transition between land and water is an awkward time for both paddler and canoe. It's hard to avoid getting wet feet when moving the canoe out of water and onto the land. There are two ways of handling this situation: wear boots and try to keep the feet dry or be prepared to get your feet wet and wade in the water. "Wet shoes" can be specially made for immersion or they can simply be an old pair of shoes that you don't mind getting wet. A pair of old runners or special sport sandals designed for this task are common choices. Some people prefer footwear that keeps their feet dry. Unfortunately, it's easy to slip off a wet log or rock at the portage and wind up with water coming in over top of the footwear. Generally the most practical option is to wear something that you don't mind getting completely wet. An option that's becoming quite popular is Gore-Tex socks.

51

With these socks, you can wear any footwear that you wish, as it's the socks that keep your feet dry, not the footwear. Even if you slip and get the socks soaked, they'll dry out quite quickly even while you're wearing them.

When the temperatures get cooler, it's important to keep the feet warm and dry. Gum-rubber boots work well for young children because they are relatively tall and can keep water away from their feet. However, because the boots slide on, they'll also slide off if they get stuck in the mud. The other problem is that rubber boots tend to be cold on the feet. Layers of good warm hydrophobic socks will help to reduce these problems.

Well-fitting and supportive shoes are important for children because their bodies are developing. Proper support for their feet will force their heels to land squarely on the ground and not tilt to either side. Adults with back and knee problems know how important proper heel placement and foot support is. Once children get settled in their walking habits, it is something that they will likely do for a lifetime so its important to try to help them with footwear that provides heel and arch support and are fitted properly.

Keeping Out the Rain

Don't scrimp on rain gear for little campers. Get quality rain gear for your child and let them try it out in advance of a trip. Have the kids test it out by running through a garden sprinkler for an hour or so. This is a task that they'll enjoy on a nice summer day.

For infants, use a poncho arrangement that covers both the child and their seat. Add an umbrella over top of them and they will continue to sleep in the canoe with no problem.

Good quality rain gear is available for toddlers and older children. Check to see how well the seams in the jacket and pants are sealed and how well the weatherproofing of the zipper openings has been done. Although waterproof breathable garments are now starting to be manufactured in children's sizes, well-sealed polyurethane-coated nylon garments for toddlers and young children will be more readily available. A quick test you can try in the store to determine how waterproof the fabric might be is to hold it tight against your lips and try to blow through it. If it's easy or doesn't have much resistance, chances are it won't be waterproof. Rain gear should be resistant to the "pucker test."

■ *Caring for rain gear*

Once the rainwear is selected, knowing how to care for the garments will help to ensure they won't fail on a canoe trip. Coated nylon rainwear can be cleaned by gentle washing but should never be put into the dryer. The coating may melt, and because it is petroleum-based, it could even ignite and start a fire. Also, keep in mind that most insect repellents are solvents and will eventually break down petroleum-based fabrics. Don't carry insect repellent in rain gear pockets. Store rain gear on hangers when not in use so that the seams don't crack.

Growing concerns

More and more outdoors retailers carry basic children's active wear. Look for clothing that will allow the child more than one year's growth before replacement is necessary. Look for adjustable elastic bands on the waist and elastic cuffs rather than plain hems on pants. This allows the child to wear the pants even when they are too long but keeps them from dragging on the ground and getting worn out. The elastic cuffs and baggy clothing also discourage bugs. Elastic waistbands that offer some adjustment will accommodate the increase in waist line diameter for the next year. Often these waistbands are in the form of an elastic belt that is partially sewn in place. Also, the material on the cuffs is important to consider. Slightly longer sleeves on a jacket can be held up with an elastic or Velcro cuff. If it is different from the fabric of the garment, check to see if it might increase the drying time of the cuff before purchasing the article. Pant cuffs will get wet and dirty and they will need to dry quickly to keep the child warm.

Fleece garments can also be purchased with multi-season and multi-year function in mind. Fleece pants and tops that contain Spandex, will allow the garment to fit loosely yet not be baggy one-year and still fit the second year. Because of the elasticity of the fabric and the hydrophobic nature of thin polyester fleece, Spandex pants and tops could be used as underwear or a base layer or for pajamas. Additional layers of various weights of fleece pants, tops and vests can help to build an insulation layer for the youngsters.

Underwear

Once an infant is out of diapers, training pants take over. Although they are often available in 100-percent cotton, training pants that are fifty-percent cotton and fifty-percent man-made fibers are a better option. They will still be less absorbent, but they will dry more quickly. Boys and girls underwear is available in cotton-polyester blends. A practical alternative to traditional underwear on camping trips is bathing-suit bottoms. Select bathing suits that are made from thin man-made fabrics, as they will provide comfortable yet quick-drying underwear.

Insects and clothes

When looking for a sun hat for your child, remember to look for one with a wide brim that will keep their face protected. The type that has an attached flap of fabric at the back can can keep the sun away from the child's ears and the back of their neck and it can also protect them from annoying bugs. If the hat doesn't have a built-in flap, a bandanna or tea towel can be tucked under the hat to accomplish the same thing.

Children seem to be a tasty treat for blackflies and mosquitoes. Bug jackets are a chemical-free alternative to commercial insect repellent. Bug jackets or shirts are available in children's sizes. They generally have tightly woven cotton or cotton-polyester hoods, backs, fronts and shoulders, with the remaining parts of the jacket made from a fine mesh. The panel of mesh that covers the face can usually be unzipped. The idea is that wherever bugs can land and the fabric is in close contact to the skin, the fabric needs to be tightly woven to prevent the bugs from being able to bite through. Elsewhere, the garment allows plenty of airflow through the mesh.

Color seems to influence bugs. It has been our experience that dark colors attract more mosquitoes and blackflies; bright colors attract more bees and wasps; deerflies seem to be attracted to movement regardless of the color; while horseflies are attracted to dark, shiny, wet-looking objects.

Lifejacket as clothing

Children should wear lifejackets (PFDs) any time they are in the canoe or near water. Besides being a safety device, a lifejacket will provide warmth, as they are made with closed-cell foam, which traps body heat. Wearing a lifejacket under a rain jacket will help trap heat in the core body areas. This retains excess heat, allowing it to circulate around the arms before it escapes through the cuffs and neck openings. As long as the lifejacket is dry, it will act as an insulator. If the lifejacket is wet, it's a better idea to put it on over top of the rain gear. This will help to provide some warmth for the core body areas. On the water the lifejacket is a lifesaving device and can keep the child warm. On land the lifejacket can provide extra warmth for the child on cold days and help protect them when they fall.

On hot, humid days the lifejacket can reduce the ability of the body to evaporate and radiate away sufficient heat. Monitoring the heat levels of your child for over- and underheating is essential. When overheating occurs, cool the child with water. Put a wet T-shirt on under the lifejacket. Wet bandannas around the neck or wrapped around the wrists of the child will also help keep them cooler. A short swim works well if the water is warm enough.

Cold weather clothes

The canoeing and camping season can continue as long as there is no ice on the rivers or lakes. Bring along winter coats for the kids. Since a toddler is still likely to get wet, have them wear the coat under a rain jacket.

Down vests and jackets were added to our boys clothing systems when they were old enough to realize the importance of keeping their coats dry. One summer we were planning one of our arctic adventures and Debra managed to find down jackets for everyone except Brendan, who was a size 6X. Being handy with sewing needle she elected to remodel Brendan's winter coat, sewing the down from one of our old coats into his kid-size nylon jacket. When all the down from the adult jacket was stuffed into the small coat, the jacket looked funny, but it became Brendan's favorite jacket even through the next winter. He called it his "puff jacket" and it kept him warm even in the Arctic.

Packing it all up

Since everything from underwear to footwear usually winds up in the same clothes bag for the canoe trip, proper packing is important. If everyone's clothes are packed together in one waterproof bag, it's inevitable that what you are looking for will be at the bottom. Instead, pack each individual's clothes separately in color-coded stuff sacks, then put these in one waterproof bag. We found that packing the kids' clothes in one waterproof bag and the adult clothing in another waterproof pack helped to reduce the problem of locating clothes. Socks and underwear seem to be the items needed most frequently. These can be packed in their own stuff sack and put at the top of the waterproof clothes packs. That makes them readily accessible without having to tear the packs apart.

What to do with dirty clothes
Keep in mind that you'll need to provide a separate place to keep dirty laundry. You don't want to mix the soiled clothes with the clean ones. The dirty laundry should be kept inside a separate waterproof pack so the odors can't escape. Ensure that everything is dried out before getting dumped into the laundry bag, this will eliminate the chances of mildew developing. If it is not possible to dry out the dirty clothing, remember to dump them onto a tarp to air out at the first available opportunity. This will help protect the other clothes from mildew damage and reduce the odor.

Diaper pail
When traveling with an infant or a toddler, use another waterproof bag just for dirty diapers. Keep this bag either clipped to the outside of a pack or packed beside the clean diapers or training pants. Wet diapers will go into this bag. Solid matter should be disposed of under moss or covered in a shallow trench so it can decompose naturally. Adding warm water and a small amount of biodegradable soap powder to this diaper bag produces an instant portable washer. Agitating the bag or letting the older kids roll it back and forth between them gets the diapers started through the wash cycle with ease. When the wash is done, just drain the water into the same area that you're using for the toilet. Rinse with clean water and the diapers are ready to be hung up to dry. Writing "diaper pail" clearly on the outside of the bag with a permanent felt-tip pen is a good way to ensure that the bag is easy to identify.

Safety considerations
Children must be well supervised when they are anywhere near the fire or the cook stove, and special care should be taken to ensure that their clothing doesn't come in contact with sparks or flying embers. Generally, natural fibers burn, but man-made fibers tend to melt when subjected to high heat. If the fabric melts onto the skin, the

burns are more serious because the melted material continues to damage the skin even after the flames are out. Keep in mind that just because a fabric has been treated with a fire-retardant finish doesn't mean that it is fireproof.

In a nutshell

Not many years ago, camping clothes were just old worn-out clothes from home. Technological advances in the textile industry have allowed manufacturers to produce garments for every family member that reduce or eliminate the discomforts of being cold or damp. This has taken camping with children from an experience to endure to an experience to enjoy and savor. If a child's early experiences are warm and dry, they'll be much happier and safer than a wet, cold child, who may lose their enthusiasm for the outdoors and never want to go camping again.

The right kind of equipment can help you deal with special situations.
This wide, stable tripping canoe meant we could run rapids on
the French River easily.

Chapter 3

....

Equipment

UNTIL RECENTLY, BEING PROPERLY OUTFITTED FOR CAMPING
meant owning a large canvas tent that leaked, a musty sleeping bag,
some surplus kitchen pots, and some worn-out street clothes. People
heading out for a camping trip often said they were going to be
"roughing it." Nowadays, manufacturers of outdoor equipment
produce gear that makes spending time in the wilderness a much safer
and more enjoyable experience.

Packs

If you're considering buying a larger pack because your current one is
jammed too full, be warned that it won't be long before the extra space
is filled with more stuff.

Packs come in a variety of styles, some more suited to canoeing than
others. External frame packs are great for hiking, but the frame makes it
hard to get the packs in and out of the canoe. Packs with an internal
frame or no frame at all are a much better choice for use in canoes.
Many packs designed for canoe-tripping now come with an internal
waterproof lining. Some have a zipper that goes around the entire front
area when the pack is lying down, allowing easy access. Packs that are
designed with canoeing in mind will often have fabric handles that
make it easier to lift the pack out of a canoe.

When we travel, everyone in the family has their own fanny pack in which to keep rain gear and some personal items, so that they are available at all times. Inside the fanny pack, we also put minimal survival equipment, such as waterproof matches, a knife, some mosquito netting to cover our hands and face, a whistle and a compass. (The kids didn't get matches or knives till they were old enough to be responsible with them.)

One of the biggest problems on camping trips is finding ways to protect your gear and food from animals and water. A significant improvement has been the introduction of large-mouthed polyethylene barrels with carrying harnesses. Two of these barrels will fit inside most canoes and still leave room for other gear. Most of these barrels have a quick snap fastener that virtually guarantees that water won't come in, even when completely submerged. Raccoons don't have a hope of accessing your food when it's stored in the barrels, and even bears would have a difficult time.

Over the years, we've found other interesting uses for the barrels. On one trip, the last section of the river became silt laden, so we scooped water into an empty barrel and let the silt settle out to obtain water that we then filtered for our use. The barrels have been used as tables and make fairly good camp chairs. We've also used them as bathtubs for our kids. On really long trips, we've found that they're a perfect height for a barber's chair. The guys take turns in the chair while Mom deftly wields the scissors.

Canoes

Canoes are the workhorse of wilderness travel. No other means of transportation is as suitable for travel in large areas of North America's wilderness. And no other way of traveling through the wilderness makes it as easy to take children along.

The first step in choosing a canoe is to carefully define what your requirements are. Does it have to be light? How much weight will be carried in the canoe? Will it be paddled by different people or will the partners be the same people all the time? Will it be used on flatwater, in whitewater, or both? Keep in mind that there is no one perfect canoe that will fill every need. Any canoe design will involve some compromise. Just be sure that you don't compromise on the things that are high priority items for your family.

Choosing a suitable canoe requires knowing a bit about the

various parts of the canoe. At first glance, canoes appear to be the same at both ends, but of course one end is the front (bow), the other is the back (stern). The easiest way to tell them apart is to look at the seats. The stern seat is smaller and placed nearer the end of the canoe, while the bow seat is wider and placed closer to the middle of the canoe. The graceful curves where the sides of the canoe come together at the front and back of the canoe are called the stems. The shape of the stem can be plumb (straight up and down) recurved (bends back towards the middle of the canoe) or flared (top is farther out than the bottom). Canoes with a flared stem tend to be drier in rough water because wave splashes are directed away from the canoe. Recurved stems produce gunwales that are narrower in the bow and stern, which makes it easier to paddle the canoe.

Canoe shapes

The part of the canoe that slices through the water at the front is called the entry line. A canoe with a sharp entry line will tend to be fast to paddle, but won't be as dry in waves and will usually be a little harder to turn. A blunt entry line will be a little slower, but will ride over waves rather than slicing through them and tend to be a little more maneuverable.

Just behind the stems are little covers called deck plates. They provide some rigidity to the stem section of the canoe and a convenient place for tying ropes or handles with which to carry the canoe for short distances. Attached to the deck plates and running down the top edge of the canoe are long strips of wood, aluminum or vinyl called gunwales (also called gunnels or rails). (The term was originally used for the place on wooden ships that carried canons.) Canoes may have a flat sheer line (the gunwale line) with an abrupt rise at the end to meet the stem, or they may have a sheer line that rises gradually from the center thwart to the stem. Flat sheer lines make a canoe a little easier to paddle because the sides of the canoe aren't as high, but raised sheer lines help to keep the paddler drier in rough water.

Beside the seats, which are attached to the inwales (inside gunwales), short canoes will have a single long, thin piece of wood called a thwart that spans the middle of the canoe. Longer canoes may also have a second thwart between the stern seat and the middle thwart. Canoes that are outfitted for solo paddling will sometimes have a special thwart

A wide, stable canoe is a good choice for family outings. Lake Superior weather changes quickly, but parents should always be prepared with extra clothes and rain shelter even on trips close to home.

that is wider, tilted a bit and lowered so that paddlers can use it to kneel against. Some canoes may have a specially sculptured thwart called a yoke in the middle. The yoke is a wide piece of wood that is shaped to fit your shoulders, with a notch in the middle for your neck. This makes it easier to carry the canoe on portages. Yokes may all look quite similar, but many of them can be uncomfortable, so it's important to try a yoke before getting one for your canoe.

When purchasing canoes, it's important to understand what some of the specifications in the catalogs mean. The greatest distance from the bow stem to the stern stem is the canoe's overall length. The length of canoe that is actually in the water when it is floating with a normal load is more important for canoeists to know and that may be different than the overall length, depending on the shape of the stem. A plumb stem will have identical waterline and overall lengths. A flared stem will have a shorter waterline length than an overall length. A recurved stem may be shorter or longer, depending on where the recurve is in relation to the waterline. A canoe with a greater overall length than the waterline length (flared stem) will tend to be more affected by the wind. It's also important to know that manufacturers don't all use the same standard when publishing their sizes. Some publish waterline lengths, some use overall length, and some use a measurement that is a compromise between the two.

The curvature of the bottom of the canoe from end to end is called the rocker. Canoes with a lot of rocker turn easily because the ends are higher out of the water, so there is less resistance to turning. Ones with little or no rocker are easier to paddle in a straight line but do not turn well. Canoes with ends that drop below the middle of the canoe are referred to as hog-backed. Because they are hard to maneuver, they are considered poor designs. The easiest way to tell how much rocker a canoe has is to put it on a level surface and have someone hold it upright. Walk back a bit and bend down to look under the canoe. It's easy to see where the rocker starts and ends by where the canoe's bottom loses contact with the ground.

The center line along the bottom of the canoe that goes from bow to stern is called the keel line. Keels are a long, thin piece of wood or metal that runs the length of the canoe. Some canoes have no keel, others have one attached, and some have a keel that is molded in. Keels are not really required on most canoes. Their original function was mainly to provide some protection for the bottoms of canvas canoes. People often assume that keels are used to keep the canoe going in a straight line. In reality, they don't have much influence on that at all. The ability of a canoe to stay on track has more to do with the shape of the hull than anything else. Keels will only have an effect if a canoe is being forced sideways through the water, such as when it's being blown by the wind or it passes over a current in a river. Some canoes were manufactured with three keels along the bottom. The extra keels will have no impact on the performance of the canoe they simply add stiffness to the bottom of the canoe.

If several different kinds of canoes were cut in half and the midsections examined, it would become apparent that there is a lot of variety in their shapes. The widest area of the canoe is called the beam. Canoes with a wider beam will be more stable and can carry more gear, but they tend to be slower. The area where the bottom of the canoe turns up to become the sides is called the chine or the bilge. If the sides of the canoe rise straight up they're called plumb, if they get wider they are called flared, and if they curve back in, tumblehome. This inward curvature means the canoeist doesn't have to reach out as far to put the paddle in the water, so it's easier on the arms. Flare-sided canoes tend to be drier in rough water and are harder to tip but require a wider reach for the paddler.

Some canoes will have quite flat bottoms, while others will have a shallow arch, and still others have a bit of a V shape. Flat-bottom canoes feel stable but tend to be slower to paddle. They don't perform well in rough water. Shallow-arch designs are the most common bottom shape in quality canoes. They tend to be fairly quick and give a predictable ride. They may feel a little tippy for novices when they first get in, but that feeling goes away quickly. A canoe with a shallow arch is actually less likely to tip than a flat-bottomed canoe in many circumstances. Canoes with a V-shaped bottoms are a compromise between a flat-bottom and a shallow-arch. They tend to ride a little deeper in the water and don't turn quite as easily, but they are generally easier to paddle in a straight line.

It's important to find a hull shape that gives you the kind of performance you want for the type of paddling you like to do. Generally, most canoes hull shapes are optimized for one of three things: speed (long, narrow canoes with little rocker and sharp entry lines); carrying capacity (wider canoes with flatter bottoms carry more gear); and maneuverability (shorter canoes with a lot of rocker feel at home in moving water).

Many canoes do all of these things reasonably well but shine most in one of the three areas. People intent on canoeing with a family will probably prefer a hull shape designed for tripping. Tripping canoes have the capacity to carry a lot of gear and are usually sixteen to eighteen feet long. Two adults, two infants and enough gear for a couple of weeks can be squeezed into a sixteen-foot canoe, but it gets a bit crowded. Adding an extra foot to the length of the canoe doesn't seem like it would make a lot of difference, but the longer canoe also becomes wider, so it will accommodate a surprising amount of extra gear. An eighteen-foot canoe will handle a lot more gear, but they tend to be a little too heavy to handle comfortably on portages and more difficult to maneuver on the water because of the extra length. A longer canoe makes it easier to travel as a family, but children are not like other loads, which remain a constant size and weight. Every year they grow a little, and eventually even an eighteen-foot canoe will be too small for a family of four. By the time our children were five years old, they were contributing enough with their paddling that we felt comfortable heading out in two sixteen-foot canoes. As long as both parents are comfortable controlling a canoe, each adult can take a stern seat while a youngster occupies the bow.

A fairly recent concept in canoe designs is the asymmetrical hull shape (the front of the canoe is a different shape than the back). Traditional canoes are identical at both ends. The asymmetrical hull is quite different at each end. This design presents some problems for families who want to involve young children in paddling. The asymmetrical shape gives some speed advantage, but we found it hard to adjust the trim of the canoe properly. Trim is the distribution of weight in a canoe. The goal is usually to have the bow of the canoe just a bit higher out of the water than the stern of the canoe. When the weight of the stern paddler is so much greater than the bow paddler (as it is when a small child is your partner), no matter how the packs are arranged, the bow is always much further out of the water than the stern.

We found it much more practical to use a traditionally shaped canoe and paddle it backwards. We'd use the narrower stern section as the bow seat for the child, and the adult would sit in the bow seat but face the back of the canoe. This made it much easier to adjust the canoe's trim. Our kids liked it a lot better because they found it much easier to paddle. The bow seats on most canoes are just too far away from the side of the canoe to allow small children to reach the water with their paddle. They always found it much cozier when they got to sit in the small (stern) seat when it was at the front of the canoe.

Picking the right canoe

Your own skill level will affect how comfortable you will feel with various canoe designs. A canoe's characteristics change as it is loaded with packs and equipment, so it's important to try out canoes when they are both empty and loaded. Borrow or rent different kinds and use them on trips to find out what canoe designs best suit your needs. If you go out on a trip with a group, ask to try out some of the other boats and ask their owners what they like and don't like about them.

Another thing that you need to determine before buying a canoe is which type of construction material best suits your needs and your pocketbook. There are six common manufacturing processes that use different materials to produce canoes in a variety of price ranges and characteristics. Many canoe models are available in several different construction materials.

■ *Traditional cedar-and-canvas*

The cedar-and-canvas canoe evolved as a European adaptation of the aboriginal birchbark canoe. Using techniques similar to those employed in shipbuilding, planks of cedar were fastened to ribs that were steamed then bent over a form. The completed hull was then covered by stretching and fastening a single piece of canvas over the canoe. The canvas was then made waterproof by the application of filler to seal the cloth. The canoe was then painted.

Cedar-and-canvas canoes have been commercially available in North America for more than a hundred years. The era of mass production of cedar-and-canvas canoes began to wane in the 1960s, mostly because of the introduction of fiberglass as a canoe construction material. By 1980 the large manufacturers of wooden canoes had closed their doors forever. Today, there are many small shops with builders who still produce limited numbers of these beautiful and durable boats. Cedar-and-canvas canoes aren't for everyone, but for the connoisseur who appreciates quality, there is no finer feeling than paddling a cedar-and-canvas canoe through the morning mist on a calm lake.

■ *Cedar-strip*

Canoes made from long, narrow strips of wood that run the entire length of the hull are known as cedar-strip canoes. They were originally made with oak ribs and relied on the tight fit of the wood strips to keep the water out. Now they are more commonly made from long strips glued to each other on a form, then sanded smooth and covered with a transparent layer of fiberglass inside and out. This produces a strong and durable canoe sometimes referred to as a cedar-glass canoe. These beautiful watercraft are made either in limited production runs by builders in small shops or by hobbyists who want to build their own canoe. This type of construction requires a minimal amount of tools and expertise. Anyone with good woodworking skills should be able to build their own cedar-glass canoe. There are a several books available to guide one through the process of strip construction. Plans are readily available and kits can be purchased that supply most of the materials.

The hull designs for many of the strip canoe models are based on the traditional cedar and canvas canoe. However, even though the designs and the basic hull shape may be similar, a cedar-strip canoe will feel different on the water. Find one and try it first, as it usually takes a month or two to complete one of these canoes, and it would be a lot of effort to invest in something you didn't like when it was finished.

Even though cedar-strip canoes appear fragile, they are much sturdier than they look. Exposure to the sun breaks down fiberglass, so the canoe should be stored under a cover when it is not in use. This is good advice for any canoe, except for those made from aluminum, which don't need protection from the sun.

The hardest part of owning a stripper canoe is the dread of getting the first scratch. Once that's out of the way, paddlers seem to be much more comfortable about using their boat for everyday use. Scratches on the hull are usually fairly easy to fix, so there really isn't any need to be worried.

■ *Aluminum*

Aluminum canoes are a post-war product that evolved from the aircraft industry. These boats were once the most common livery or rental canoe and can still be found by the score on the racks of most rental facilities, though they have become less popular in recent years. While they require almost no maintenance, they are noisy to paddle and get hot in the sun or cold when the water is cold.

In their heyday, they were often used for whitewater paddling because they would bend instead of break when they hit rocks. Some of the new plastic materials are much more suitable for this type of paddling. Aluminum tends to stick to rocks instead of sliding over them. This results in a sudden, abrupt halt of forward movement. From personal experience, this can be quite painful because when the canoe stops, there's a tendency for the person who's paddling it to continue in the direction of travel.

■ *Fiberglass*

The introduction of fiberglass in canoe construction had a major impact on the popularization of the sport because it brought the price of canoes down to the point where they were affordable for almost anyone. Currently there are probably more fiberglass canoes in production than all other types of construction combined. New paddlers often choose fiberglass canoes because of their availability and affordability. Fiberglass canoes are also among the easiest to repair and require little maintenance. Though there's no reason why a good fiberglass canoe can't provide the family with good service for many years, most people who continue with paddling usually exchange their fiberglass canoes for ones made from one of the other materials as their needs evolve.

There are a lot of good canoe designs made in fiberglass, but it's just as easy to make a bad design as a good one. Before buying a fiberglass canoe it is especially important to paddle ones of several different shapes and styles to be certain that the one you select suits your needs.

■ *Kevlar and specialty cloth*

If weight is a consideration, Kevlar or some of the new specialty-cloth constructions are attractive options. The techniques used to build canoes with these materials are similar to those used in good-quality fiberglass construction, but they are a lot more expensive. Generally, because they do cost more to make and sell, manufacturers tend to research their hull shapes more carefully. That means that its less likely that poorly shaped canoes will make their way into full-scale production.

While the super lightweight canoes are a joy to carry on a portage, their light weight makes them hypersensitive on the water. When children are in the canoe, this may be a disadvantage, as heavier canoes will certainly be more stable. As well, manufacturers often make their lightweight canoes in "fast" hull shapes. The faster, sleeker designs usually sacrifice a little stability to achieve speed. Kevlar and the other lightweight materials are becoming popular with people who do a lot of wilderness tripping. They are strong and durable and so light, they can almost make portages fun.

■ *ABS and other plastics*

The introduction of plastics revolutionized the plumbing industry by providing pipe material that was strong, flexible and easy to form into unusual shapes. It wasn't long before it began showing up in all sorts of places, including canoes. To make a canoe from ABS (acrylonitrile-butadiene-styrene) a large sheet composed of a five-layer laminate is

Accommodating scaled-down paddlers requires some adaptations. Turning the canoe around means the weight is distributed better and the child will find it easier to reach the water with their shorter arms.

heated until it is soft enough to be forced into a mold. Once this cools down and the seats, thwarts and gunwales are added, it becomes a durable craft that is low in maintenance and almost indestructible. Canoes made from ABS are preferred by people looking for a tough, long-lasting canoe to paddle in whitewater or to take on long wilderness trips.

ABS isn't the only plastic material that canoes are made from. There are a few canoe designs made from polyethylene, the same material that freezer and microwave food containers are made from. Polyethylene canoes tend to be a little heavier and don't keep their shape as well as ABS canoes do, but they are less expensive and more abrasion-resistant.

We've been on several trips where we have seen ABS canoes folded entirely in half around a rock in a strong current. After the canoes were pulled off the rock, they popped back to their original shape with only few wrinkles in the hull to show where the folds once were.

We generally use our ABS canoes more often than any of the others. They are a bit on the heavy side to carry, but we find them most suitable for our purposes. Not all ABS canoes are heavy. Our boys have their own twelve-foot ABS canoe that only weighs thirty-two pounds.

■ *Folding canoes*

Folding canoes made from the same type of tough material used on whitewater rafts have been used in Europe for quite some time, but they're starting to become more common here. The advantage to these canoes is that they take so little space for storage. When they're folded up, they are not much larger than big sack full of laundry. A folded canoe qualifies as one piece of checked luggage on commercial airlines, which means they can solve some of the difficult logistical problems in accessing remote wilderness routes.

We used folding Pakboat canoes on our most recent arctic trip and were pleased that we did. The canoes took a bit to get used to, as they handled a little differently than we were accustomed to, but they were certainly rugged enough and there were no problems with them being able to handle the heavy loads. We brought the canoes with us on commercial flights to Inuvik as baggage, and all of our gear — and canoes — fit inside the bushplane on the trip to the river.

Paddles

Choosing a paddle that's right for you will depend on what you plan to use it for and the level of skill you've developed. There are specialized paddles for racing, for whitewater, for stylized paddling and for tripping. Paddles can be handcarved from select pieces of hardwood or they can be mass-produced by machine from laminated pieces of wood reinforced with artificial materials. One of the most versatile and popular paddles is made from a solid piece of hardwood. Most canoeists own more than one paddle and often take more than one on a trip. It is fairly common to see paddlers use a solid or laminated wooden paddle for traveling distances, then switch to a plastic-bladed paddle in shallow water or rapids.

One of the most important considerations when selecting a paddle is its weight. If an average stroke rate is about thirty per minute, that makes 1,800 strokes an hour and 14,400 strokes in an eight-hour day. An average wooden paddle can weigh about two pounds. If we add up the number of times that two pounds has been lifted, we come to the staggering realization that the canoeist has lifted 28,800 pounds of wood during the day. Shaving even a small amount of weight off a paddle can make a big difference in how tired the arms feel at the end of the day.

For general-purpose use, a traditional beaver-tail-shaped paddle will probably be the most comfortable. This style of paddle has been used for centuries. Normally, the blade should be narrower than the greatest distance that you can span with your hand when you stretch out your thumb and little finger. A wider paddle is likely to feel more tiring to use. It's common to have paddles vary a little bit in shaft diameter and its worth trying several to see if thicker or thinner shafts feel more comfortable in your hands.

To check a standard paddle for overall length, the grip of the paddle should come somewhere between your nose and the top of your shoulders when the tip of the paddle is resting on the ground. People who have more experience paddling will often have different length preferences for different types of canoeing. There aren't any firm guidelines, it's just a question of what feels most comfortable for the individual who is going to use the paddle.

Children outgrow their paddles quickly. Because they are so short, their paddles should be longer in proportion to their bodies than for adults. Using adult guides to select a paddle for a child may result in them not being able to reach the water when they're in a canoe. Light weight is probably the single most important criteria in choosing a paddle for a child. Involve the child in the selection of their paddle and be flexible about their choices. Putting decals or drawings on the paddle can get kids to take a greater interest in using it.

Adults should never assume that kids won't want to paddle on a trip. When our younger boy was two and a half, he and his brother came with us on a trip down the White River to Lake Superior. We brought a paddle for his older brother, who was five, but didn't bring one for the youngster. It wasn't long into the trip before it became apparent that our omission was going to cause trouble. Watching his older brother use a paddle, the younger one felt left out. Soon after the trip began, an evening was spent using an ax and a knife to shape a paddle out of a piece of driftwood. Once the paddle was constructed, we had peace for the rest of the trip. Brendan still has this paddle in his room and still finds pleasure in playing with it from time to time.

Lifejackets

Commonly referred to as lifejackets, there must be an approved personal floatation device (PFD) of the appropriate size for every occupant in a canoe. There is a difference between a lifejacket and a PFD. Lifejackets are designed to roll an unconscious person face up and keep their heads out of the water, while a PFD will simply keep a person afloat. The collar on children's lifejackets helps to keep the child's head out of the water.

Current laws in most parts of North America don't require canoeists to wear their lifejackets. Some adults choose to wear theirs all the time, others choose to wear them only when conditions are rough. The level of risk that an adult is willing to accept often depends on their ability to swim and the weather and river conditions. Good lifejackets are comfortable enough to wear all the time. Parents should never take chances with their children's welfare. They should be in their lifejackets any time they're near or on the water. The only exception would be in controlled situations such as when they are swimming or playing in shallow water under direct parental supervision.

All lifejackets are rated for the weight they are designed to support. Besides making sure the weight rating is appropriate, it's important to be sure that the lifejacket fits properly. For children, it's important that the lifejacket have a strap that goes under the crotch to keep it from sliding off. Properly fitted lifejackets are snug under the ribs, which helps keep them from riding up. Over the last few years, several manufacturers have started producing models made specifically to fit women. A properly fitted lifejacket makes it easier to wear the safety device while paddling.

Tents

Choose a tent that meets your family's requirement for shelter, that is light enough to carry, easy to set up and affordable. It is possible to rent tents and that's a good place to start if you're not sure of what you need in a tent. Keep in mind that toddlers can be hard on tents because they're too young to understand that they can't lean on tent walls. As well, their balance isn't that great and they'll sometimes simply stumble onto the sides of the tent accidentally. Even though they're small, they still weigh enough to do damage. Durable tents are important during the toddler phase.

As long as youngsters feel comfortable in a canoe, they usually make excellent travelers. They should have their own paddle, a few toys and a comfortable place to nap. Infants should have a seat so they can see what's going on around them.

Travel by canoe is an excellent way to provide youngsters with an opportunity to see wildlife. This Algonquin Park moose is accustomed to canoeists and isn't threatened by a close approach, but it's important to be sensitive to the behavior of animals, and to make sure they aren't disturbed by your presence, for their safety and yours.

The wilderness is a natural classroom, but it helps to come prepared with a few tools to make sure kids get the most out of the experience. Binoculars, a magnifying glass and some age-appropriate guidebooks should be included in the pack whenever possible.

It's not always easy to rouse children in the morning, but that's often the best time to see wildlife. The quiet morning air made it easy to hear the snorts and whistling sounds this white-tailed deer made on its way across the meadow.

While on a lunch break, young Kyle took an unusually strong interest in this paddle. As it turned out, he was cutting his first tooth. Since he didn't want to give up the paddle, we cleaned it with soap and rinsed it with sterile water to protect him against germs.

Youngsters often want to be independent and paddle a canoe by themselves. Unfortunately, they lack the skill to bring a canoe back once they're away from shore. A long rope tied between the canoe and a tree can keep them within a safe distance.

Small children lose body heat faster than adults do. Warm clothes that don't absorb water, a hat and warm waterproof boots are important items to bring camping. Providing them with nutritious food that they like to eat will also help keep them warm.

It's impossible to avoid dirt on a camping trip and dirt is like a magnet to children. Bringing along a tarp for the kids to play on can lessen the exposure to dirt, and dressing them in clothes that are easy to clean makes it easier to deal with the problem.

The need to cuddle can happen anywhere and a long portage is an awkward place to deal with it. You wouldn't want to try this without having lots of experience carrying packs, but in this case it helped.

On a trip down the White River to Lake Superior, we didn't bring a paddle for Brendan because we thought he was too young. Along the way, we had to carve him this paddle from driftwood. He used it for several years.

The south coast of Newfoundland has some spectacular scenery and great beaches. Even though it was warm, we dressed the kids' upper bodies in warm clothes to protect against cool ocean breezes. Shorts and sandals helped limit the amount of salt being brought into the tent.

On a quiet October morning in Killarney Provincial Park, the landscape is shrouded in mist as the cool air hangs over the warm water. Since the days are shorter, it's easier to rouse children to admire the sunrise.

Colors might not seem like an important consideration, but it's amazing how much more cheery it is to wake up inside a tent with bright colors. Yellow and blue are our favorites because they give the feeling of warm sunshine and blue sky. That's a much nicer way to start the day if the morning is really gray and drizzling.

Tall tents are nice and roomy, so they are attractive for family use. The downside is that tall tents are more vulnerable to strong winds. A good compromise height is one that allows an adult's head to clear the ceiling while they are kneeling. Smaller tents are also more likely to feel warmer because there is less air inside them to heat up.

Most tents are made of synthetic materials such as polyester or nylon. These tightly woven materials don't breathe. The moisture contained in the occupant's breath and from their perspiration doesn't pass easily from inside the tent to the outside. If the tent isn't well ventilated, it can feel clammy inside because of the perspiration condensing on things inside.

Good tents have ceilings made from a breathable material, sometimes with mesh panels in it. On well thought-out designs, these panels have zippered coverings to permit adjustments to the amount of ventilation. To keep the inside dry, there is a second, outer ceiling called a fly that goes over top of the tent. Tents should be designed to allow air to circulate under the fly and wick away the condensation inside. Tents whose fly doesn't cover the entire outside area may be okay for backyard camping but shouldn't be used in the wilderness. The entrance to the tent should be designed in such a way that rain doesn't get inside when the doors are opened to let people in and out. Many tents may have an extended fly that goes beyond the tent. This is called a vestibule and it greatly reduces the problem of rain getting in when people enter and exit the tent.

On trips where there are a few days of uninterrupted rain, you'll find that a roomy tent is a lifesaver. Having enough room to stretch out for playtime is essential to keeping young children happy when it's too miserable to be outside. It won't be possible to avoid going outside occasionally, so it's wise to look for a tent with a vestibule area where damp clothes and boots can be removed before going inside the tent. Vestibules are a great place to store gear away from the weather.

Good tent bottoms are built in what's called a bathtub construction. They have a thicker, more durable floor material that comes up the walls of the tent about six inches. The seams on the tent bottom should be covered with a waterproof tape material. Regardless of how well the bottom is made, it needs to be protected. Tent bottoms that are subjected to a lot of abuse and are liable to start leaking over time. We put a tarp under the tent before pitching it, to protect it from punctures or scrapes, then we also use a sheet of polyethylene inside to add extra protection. The polyethylene is readily available from building supply stores, where it is sold as vapor barrier material. Just stretch out enough inside the tent to make a bathtub of the material and cut off the excess where it begins to come up the walls.

Preventing punctures and scrapes and keeping the tent floor well waterproofed is essential with little ones. When our kids were young we would start every season by making a new polyethylene "tub." We always brought the sheet and the tarp along because keeping the kids warm and dry is important. The inner liner would be laid out neatly, then the sleeping pads would be laid on top to keep the plastic from moving or bunching.

The quality of zippers is also an important consideration. Zippers are great when they work, but a broken zipper on a camping trip can be a nightmare. Young children are not often adept at using zippers, so it's not a bad idea to attach short strings or ribbons to make them easier to open and close. If a zipper becomes stiff, a little lubrication with candle wax, general-purpose oil or Vaseline can make the mechanism operate as smoothly as new. If the zipper doesn't stay closed, chances are that the clasp is starting to wear out. Pinching the clasp mechanism together a bit with pliers may solve that problem.

Freestanding tents are most practical. They are usually assembled with poles that are shock-corded together so there's no chance of assembling them wrong. For a tent with poles of different sizes, we've found that its a good idea to code the various sizes of poles by putting different colors of tape on them.

Assembled poles usually either slide through sleeves or are fastened with clips to give the tent its shape and structure. This usually doesn't take a lot of time to assemble, but doing it for the first time while on a trip is not a good idea. Make sure you've assembled the tent a few times in your backyard, where time doesn't matter.

Most new tents require the application of a chemical seam sealer to ensure the waterproofing of the seams. Your backyard is also a good place to do that. Once the seam sealer is dry, you can test it with a garden sprinkler to see how well the tent sheds water. While you've got the tent set up, you might as well take the opportunity to try out your sleeping arrangements, just to be sure that everything will fit inside the tent the way you expect it to when you start using it on trips.

Dining shelters

If you have an old tent that you've been thinking about getting rid of, you may want to keep it. We've used older tents as dining shelters when the bugs are at their worst. The best dining shelter tents are ones with large windows on all four sides. It tends to get warm inside the shelter when it's filled with people eating and a good breeze helps. The dining tent doesn't need a fly, so that can be left at home to make the tent lighter and smaller to pack. You might also want to consider cutting out sections of the floor to further reduce the weight and bulk. Just be sure you don't cut out anything that's structural on the bottom.

Dining shelter tents can also be practical, safe places to take care of really small children. If it's to be used as a playpen, the tent needs a bottom. Put a tarp under it if you've already modified the floor.

Another use that we found for an old A style tent was as a rain shelter. To make the shelter lighter and smaller to pack, we cut the bottom out of it. If it looked like rain, we'd suspend the tent as high as we could between two trees. The bottom part of the A frame would be stretched out with cord attached to trees or rocks and would usually be off the ground by a foot or two. This arrangement provided a dry and fairly sheltered place to cook, eat and let the children play. We'd pitch the old tent up high enough that several people could stand under this shelter.

Sleeping equipment

When our children were about three years old, they'd often have make-believe camping adventures around the house. We first noticed it when our older son started carrying an empty laundry basket over his head. When asked what he was up to, he said he was carrying a canoe on a portage just like Mom and Dad. We seized this opportunity to enhance their camping skills. Most department stores sell kids' tents and we bought one for each of our boys. The tents were small enough to be set up in their rooms and would even fit on top of their beds. They'd often camp out in their rooms, sometimes on the floor, sometimes on their beds. This helped to make them feel more comfortable with the idea of sleeping in tents when we'd camp outdoors.

There are three components for a good night's sleep in the outdoors: a good sleeping bag, a pad to keep you off the ground, and a pillow.

The easiest way to get a good pillow is to stuff some clothes into a fuzzy polar fleece sweater or pair of pants. There are some commercially available camp pillows, but if you know anybody that's good with a sewing machine, it's just as easy to sew up a small stuff sack from polar fleece and use that to fill with clothes. This takes up less space in a pack.

The body can lose a lot of heat during a night spent sleeping on the cold ground. To prevent this from happening, it is necessary to use a pad of some sort underneath the sleeping bag. The best sleeping pads are made from something that has some cushioning for comfort but has enough resistance to keep the body from making contact with the ground and does not allow internal air to circulate. An air mattress might seem like a perfect solution, but they don't work that well. Good sleeping pads need to trap air. Foam is a better insulator than an ordinary air mattress because the air doesn't move as easily from warm body to cold ground. Ordinary foam works reasonably well, but the dampness from the ground seeps through eventually. Good pads are made from closed-cell foam that traps air in tiny bubbles throughout the foam. Unfortunately, the closed-cell pads tend to be fairly stiff and don't compress much. To make them manageable in packs, they are usually made fairly thin.

Manufacturers found an even better way of keeping the air trapped and providing a much softer pad by enclosing a piece of ordinary foam inside an airtight, watertight fabric covering with a valve on it. This type of pad can be deflated to a small diameter when not needed or blown up to full size for sleeping. Because they are filled with foam, they'll actually inflate themselves once the valve is opened; just leave them alone for about fifteen minutes.

Parents should be prepared to think of ways to keep their children from rolling while they sleep. We put things under the outside edges of their pads to make a bit of a bowl shape, which encouraged the kids to roll back to the center of their sleeping pads. As long as the lifejackets are dry, they can be used as extra padding around the kids to keep them in place. Lifejackets are made from closed-cell foam, so they're an excellent insulator. Be careful to tuck in loose straps.

The last element to a good night's sleep is a warm sleeping bag. Sleeping bags made specifically for children are becoming more common. Most of the expense in producing sleeping bags is in the labor, so it's not surprising that children's bags are often almost as expensive as adult bags. Because of the rate at which children grow, parents are inclined to buy sleeping bags with lots of room for growth. There are two reasons for concern with this practice. First, there's a risk that a really young child might smother if they roll down inside the bag. The other problem is that bags that are too large permit excessive circulation of air, which accelerates the loss of heat. Try to find sleeping bags that are as close as possible to the correct size. A sleeping bag that is a little too big for the child can be used if the excess portion is tied off so your child cannot squirm too far down. If your child is a tummy sleeper, putting a small piece of Ensolite under their chest and head area will keep their breathing unobstructed. Too much puffy material under a sleeping baby could interfere with a baby's breathing.

Down is one of the best insulators available in sleeping bags, but it is not the best choice for youngsters. A child's sleeping bag should filled with a synthetic insulation. This will avoid allergy problems, but more importantly synthetic fabrics maintain some of their insulation value even when they are wet. This is important, as the occasional overnight accident is inevitable. If necessary, portions of the sleeping bag can be washed and will probably be dried out by bedtime, especially on sunny days.

Sleeping bags are rated for their comfort zone, the lowest temperature at which the insulation can continue to retain the body's heat. The lower the number that the bag is rated for, the warmer the sleeping bag will be. These ratings are an approximate guide and parents should think about how their kids normally sleep at home when deciding what range would be suitable for their children. If your child needs more blankets to sleep at home than anyone else does, you should look for a sleeping bag with a temperature rating that's colder than what you will be expecting to actually encounter.

To extend the warmth of the bags we used polar fleece sleepers for our children. To keep sleeping bags clean, we found that it is a good idea to pack separate clothes for bedtime. These bedclothes were usually lightweight or fleece tops and bottoms that pack easily and add little bulk.

Parents should check sleeping bags for loose strings that might entangle a child. Many sleeping bags have drawstrings that are used to tighten up openings and prevent warm air from escaping. Make sure that the excess cord won't wrap around the child while they sleep.

To reduce the size of sleeping bags and clothing sacks, it's not a bad idea to look for special compression stuff sacks. These have a strap arrangement that's used to greatly reduce the size of the pack once everything has been stuffed into them.

Keeping it dry
It's important to make sure that sleeping bags and clothing don't get wet on a camping trip. They can be kept in one of the waterproof plastic barrels. There are also soft-sided canoe packs available made from waterproof material and with a roll-down waterproof top. Some fabric packs come with waterproof liners that have a roll-down tops. Various sizes of stuff sacks are made from waterproof material and have roll-down closures. Another alternative, not quite as waterproof, is to simply put a plastic bag inside all the stuff sacks and twist the opening closed before pulling the drawstring tight.

Stoves and fire
Stoves come in quite a variety of shapes and sizes. Some use solid fuel, some use a liquid fuel, and others use compressed gas. For family use, it's important to make sure that the stove you take can prepare the meals you've planned in a reasonable amount of time. Children seem to get hungry quickly on camping trips and often get cranky if it takes too long to feed them. Depending on the type of meals you've planned, that may mean taking a two-burner stove, two backpacking stoves or combining the use of a fire with a stove.

Solid-fuel stoves don't take much space but don't burn as hot as those that use liquid fuels. It's also harder to be sure of how much fuel you'll use. They are more suited to heating things up than cooking.

Compressed-gas stoves are easy to light, burn hot and clean, and are safe to use around children, as there is no liquid gas that children can get into. The canisters of gas are usually not refillable, which means you may wind up with a large collection of partly used bottles at home because you always take new ones on trips to be sure you don't run out. If your children have been learning about landfill and waste disposal at school, you may be asked some embarrassing questions about the spent

Food always tastes better outdoors, but fresh baked bread hot out of a reflector oven is hard to top. These ovens can be purchased, but we made this one from sheets of aluminum bent in a vise. The ovens fold flat when not in use.

fuel canisters. As with any garbage, if it can't be disposed of by burning, it should come back with you for proper disposal at a landfill site.

We prefer stoves that use Naphtha (also called white gas or Coleman fuel). We purchase Naphtha in large four-liter containers at the beginning of the camping season and pour it into smaller refueling bottles to bring on our trips., Keep young children away while refilling the stove with fuel. Be sure that fuel canisters can't possibly be confused with any drink containers you might use. Children may not notice the difference and try to drink from the wrong container if their drink bottle looks anything like the fuel container.

Most stoves burn with a flame that is nearly invisible, especially in the daytime. It is important to establish safety rules for children. Set a perimeter around the cooking area that the kids shouldn't cross when food is being prepared. Keep the stove packed away unless it's in use, and make it a rule that the kids shouldn't handle the stove any time its out of the container. When our kids were young, we would often cover the stove with a large overturned pot after it was turned off, so the kids couldn't touch it while we let it cool. Our boys knew that if the pot and the stove were together they were hot and they stayed away from it.

Using fires for warmth and cooking is a common practice on camping trips. Open fires are practical, but they're also one of the greatest risks to young children in the outdoors. There's also a chance that an improperly built fire could get out of hand and start a forest fire. As more people go out into the wilderness, the ethics of using fires becomes an issue. The only way to practice no-trace camping with fires is to travel with a portable firebox. This is a folding steel container that prevents the fires from damaging the rocks or soil at campsites.

A technique that is becoming popular is the use of a mini wood stove made from a large can or old cooking pot. Holes are cut in the bottom and top to feed wood in and let air circulate. The pot or frying pan used for cooking is placed at the top of the mini stove, where the heat from the wood fire is sufficient for fairly quick cooking. As long as there's a good supply of twigs at hand, this can be an effective and environmentally friendly way of cooking.

Most campsites in traveled areas will already have a fireplace that should be used if you'd like to have a fire. Unfortunately, many campers don't take proper care of the campfire area, leaving partially burnt logs and garbage. Campers should only put things in the fire that they're sure will be completely burned before they're ready to leave. All remnants in the fireplace should be reduced to white ash before leaving a campsite. Any unburned garbage should be taken out of the fireplace and brought out for disposal, even if it isn't yours. Before retiring for the night or before leaving a campsite, it is imperative that the fire is completely put out.

Water filters
The water on most wilderness trips will probably look clean and inviting to drink, but it's important to keep in mind that it may contain parasites or disease-carrying agents no matter how clean it looks or how

remote the location. Getting sick isn't fun on a weekend trip, but the consequences on an extended wilderness trip are severe enough that it's not worth taking chances. This is especially true when traveling with young children. Many waterborne parasites and diseases have a long incubation period before a problem is noticed. Severe flu-like symptoms that show up in late fall may have come from a contaminant that was encountered on a summer canoe trip. Anytime you experience flu-like symptoms after camping, it would be a good idea to let your doctor know, so they can check for waterborne illnesses.

The traditional way to purify water is to put it on a stove or fire and heat it till it's been subjected to a rolling boil for at least five minutes. Unfortunately, that isn't always practical.

Another method of purification is to bring along iodine or halazone tablets. These work quite well to prevent most illness, but they do tend to add a strong flavor to the water and it may not completely purify.

Water filters are the fastest and most reliable method of obtaining safe water. The water is forced through several filters that are designed to remove increasingly smaller particles until all that's left is clean water with a few traces of dissolved minerals that are quite safe to drink. Some filters also include active ingredients that destroy contaminants. The effectiveness of filters is measured by the smallest diameter of particle that they can extract. The unit of measurement is in microns and the smaller the number, the more effective the filter will be. Generally, the better filters tend to cost more. Most pumps use replaceable filters and it's important to follow the manufacturer's recommendations for cleaning and replacement. Bring along a spare filter for long trips.

When traveling with children, it is especially important to purify the drinking water for safety reasons. It is equally important to follow through on all areas relating to consumable water. Don't rinse dishes or toothbrushes in untreated water. There's no sense in being careful about preparing drinking water unless all sources of water that are transferred to your mouth are also treated. Filter *all* water.

Repair kit
The kind of repair kit that you pack will depend on the gear that makes up your camping outfit. Here are some general guidelines that may help you in preparing the kit.

Make sure that you've got a interchangeable-head screwdriver, and enough spare nuts and screws so that critical ones can be easily replaced if necessary. A small section of stainless steel or brass wire can be handy, and some good parachute cord can often hold things together when screws give out.

Nicks in paddle grips can cause blisters unless they're attended to, so bring some sandpaper or a piece of steel wool to take care of rough edges.

The singlemost important item in a paddler's repair kit is probably a roll of duct tape. This tough tape sticks to almost anything, is rugged and is quite waterproof. It should be applied to clean, dry surfaces, and it's not a bad idea to warm up the tape over a match before applying it if it's cold out. We remove the cardboard core from inside the duct tape rolls, which lets us squash it into a smaller package that is much easier to pack.

All camping equipment should be checked out before a trip begins, and the stove should be tested for proper functioning. Many stoves have a pump mechanism to pressurize the fuel. These pumps often require an occasional drop of oil to ensure a good seal, otherwise the pump doesn't work. On a long trip the oil may dry out and the pump won't work. We bring along a small packet of oil in case this happens, though cooking oil or even margarine can get the pump working again if nothing else is available, but these should only be used in emergencies, as they can gum up the pump.

Occasionally filler funnels for stoves get lost or forgotten. A temporary replacement can be fashioned from a piece of tinfoil.

A small sewing kit is a worthwhile addition to the repair kit. Some sewing jobs to repair camping gear involves working with thick materials. An ordinary needle and thread may not be up to the job, so it's worth looking into a sewing kit designed for outdoor repairs. Most of these come with a holding device for heavy-duty needles that will make it easier and safer to stitch thick material. Bring along a few patches that can be used for patching nylon fabrics.

When a strap from a pack breaks, even a heavy-duty needle will be hopelessly inadequate. There is a tool called a stitching awl that can handle these types of sewing repairs with relative ease. They use a heavy-duty waxed nylon cord that's run through a robust needle attached to a wooden handle that fits nicely in the palm of the hand. The stitching awl will even sew an overlapped leather strap together if one should happen to break. There are some repairs that just can't be done in the field without this tool.

A Swiss Army knife with a good assortment of gadgets is handy to include in the repair kit. One of the most indispensable tools that we've found on our knives is the small screwdriver, which is usually stored wound up inside the corkscrew. This is the perfect size to tighten the screws in eyeglasses. The scissors attachment on Swiss Army knives has also proven to be useful.

We usually bring along small quantities of several types of glue on longer trips, but if we were limited to just one, it would be five-minute epoxy. A small tube of silicone seal can handle many glue jobs on things that need to remain flexible, and it can also be used to seal leaks. Since there's always a risk of packs being squished on a camping trip, we put the glue inside a rigid container to give it extra protection.

Plastic bags are something that we usually bring along in our repair kit. They don't take much space, but they can be useful for a variety of things. We've used large plastic bags to make an emergency rain poncho for the kids and we've used small plastic bags inside their boots to give them extra waterproofing for their feet. Plastic bags can also be used inside stuff sacks to make the contents more waterproof. We even keep a bag inside the camera bag to protect it against unexpected rainfall.

Saws and hatchets

A saw is a versatile tool to bring along on extended camping trips. Besides its obvious use in cutting up wood for fires, saws can be used to make or adjust all sorts of things to make camp life safer or more comfortable. From first-hand experience, we know that it's by far the best tool to fashion a replacement for a thwart that broke while carrying a canoe across a portage.

The best types of saws are the ones that form either a triangle or a rectangle when assembled, but which come apart and fold up inside their own handles when not in use. The folded size is about the diameter of the O made when you form a circle with your thumb and your index finger, and are about as long as your forearm. There are other types of saws that are smaller when folded, but many don't cut well.

Another saw that we've found quite useful for many things is the one available in Swiss Army knives or multi-purpose tools such as the

Leatherman. There have been a few occasions when an emergency replacement tent part was constructed from wood with the tools found inside the Swiss Army knife, and the saw blade made the job so much easier.

In our opinion, hatchets should never come on a camping trip. A hatchet handle is too short to be used safely. They require a lot of care because the arc ends at about the person's shin if the swing misses. A lightweight axe is much safer.

There was a time when we were quite minimalist and brought neither ax nor saw; we'd simply gather smaller pieces of wood that could be easily broken by hand. Gathering firewood this way doesn't leave scars around campsites and it makes it easier for young children to contribute when it's time to set up camp. At one campsite we managed to luck into some long, well-dried pieces of oak that had broken from a large tree during a recent windstorm. Oak is one of the most desirable woods for campfires as it burns clean, long and hot. It also leaves a great bed of coals for cooking. We were thrilled to find this treasure.

Getting the right stuff is not easy

A lot of the equipment currently available is general purpose gear that can be used for a variety of camping experiences, but there is a trend toward more specialized equipment. This makes it more of a challenge for parents to pick the right gear for their children.

When we began tripping, we used our old cedar-and-canvas canoe for everything from a quiet day paddle in the nearby swamp to wilderness trips that spanned several weeks and included a lot of whitewater. Today, we have two canoes that we use for most trips, but there are six others on the racks in the backyard, which are more specialized designs. We could still use a cedar-and-canvas canoe for all our paddling excursions, but the specialty canoes allow us to focus more on the trip rather than worrying about the equipment. It's not that the canvas canoe was too fragile, it's just that some of the new materials require almost no maintenance. With a family, time is valuable.

All of the variety in equipment makes it even more important that you choose the right gear for your needs. Fortunately, there are lots of places that offer rental programs, which provides the opportunity to try before you buy. Stores specializing in outdoor adventure gear usually have good, well-informed staff who can assist you in selecting gear to suit most needs. It pays to ask lots of questions.

Whatever you choose to take with you, be sure that you have the materials and tools in your repair kit to rectify any problems you may encounter on the trail.

Young children need to eat more often than adults do, so parents need to make appropriate adjustments to their traveling schedule. Hot food that they like to eat is important on cold days.

Chapter 4

....

The Well-Fed Camper

*I*MAGINE TWELVE RAVENOUS ADULTS, SPOONS IN HAND, HUNKERED down around a partially consumed jar of peanut butter, the only remaining food on the last day of a six-day camping trip. This trip had been organized by a professional outfitter: "Don't worry, we've been doing this for years." Even though the trip was only six days long, it was wet and much cooler than normal. The body needs more nutrients and calories in these circumstances. As we grew thinner over those six days, the importance of having suitable quantities of good food became clear. The right food at the right time can be a lifesaver — or at least a tripsaver.

Regardless of age, the human body needs proper food for energy and for the growth and repair of tissue. Food provides our bodies with the six essential nutrients: carbohydrates, fiber, proteins, vitamins and minerals, fat, and water.

Yes, fat. In today's society, fat is considered to be something to be avoided, yet it is an essential nutrient. North American diets generally contain an excessive amount of fat, but on a canoeing or camping trip, it may be necessary to plan to include fats on the menu. Many camp meals are made from dried or packaged foods that contain only a minimal amount of fat. Canoeing and hiking burn a lot of energy, so it's important to eat foods that provide a lasting source of energy, like fat. Adding some margarine or oil to the dried or packaged food will increase the fat content, will make you feel more full after eating, and will give you more lasting energy. Carbohydrates also give us energy and are predominantly found in grains and cereals. The fiber provided in whole-grain foods helps to reduce blood cholesterol levels and to keep the bowels regular.

Our daily intake of food must also include enough water to replace the amount lost through perspiration and the elimination of waste. When we exercise or are exposed to wind and sun, our body's water requirement increases. Some of the water we need comes from the foods we eat, but the majority must come in the form of fluids we drink. Being dehydrated can affect your judgment and can be life-threatening. It is crucial to have clean, safe drinking water on hand at all times.

Just as you would at home, plan camp meals that include foods from all four food groups. Start with a list of family favorites that contain something from each food group. If a child won't eat stewed beets at home, they won't eat it on a camping trip, either.

Storage

One of the problems with camping trips is that you can't always take along favorite meals because they can't be stored properly. Correct storage is necessary to avoid food-borne illnesses. Without the comforts of home — oven, microwave and refrigerator — it may be harder to prepare meals safely in the wild. It is important to make sure the food you take camping is not only nutritious, but is also safe to eat. Foods naturally contain bacteria and microorganisms. Most bacteria are not harmful to us in small quantities. However, given the right growing conditions they can be.

For centuries our ancestors preserved foods without the convenience of modern appliances. To do this they simply reduced or eliminated the conditions for bacterial growth. Bacteria are picky eaters. They like foods that are not too sweet, not too salty, and not too acidic. Great-grandma would preserve beets and cucumbers, onions and other vegetables by pickling them in a brine of saltwater and vinegar. Fruits were often laced with lots of sugar and a little bit of ascorbic acid as they were stewed on the cookstove then poured into jars for preserves, jams or jellies. Large quantities of sugar, salt or acid make food unattractive to bacteria. Great-grandpa would generously cover fish with salt and leave it for days on drying racks until the moisture was drawn out with the aid of the salt and the sun. This was similar to the techniques used by the aboriginal people on this continent for centuries. Removing moisture from food can also prevent bacterial growth.

Fortunately, it is relatively easy to prepare safe, nourishing foods. Bulk food stores and grocery stores can supply everything we need. If cost is an issue (as it is with many families with young children), you can prepare your own foods with a little time and effort.

Many parks prohibit cans and bottles. Some people simply pour the can's contents into a reusable plastic container. This is a dangerous practice because once a can is opened, the contents must be used immediately or refrigerated to reduce bacterial growth.

Bulk food stores offer a wide variety of options, from dried vegetable flakes, dried fruits and milk powders, to dried soup and chili mixes. Grocery stores often carry other possibilities, such as beef jerkies, pasta, rice, cereals and breads. "Jerked" meats have been salted, sometimes seasoned or smoked, then dried. Beef jerky therefore is simply beef that has been dried or "jerked." More and more retailers are beginning to carry beef jerky and other dried meats.

Outdoor stores also carry a good selection of dried and freeze-dried foods. These prepackaged foods, though they may be more expensive, offer a simple alternative to planning meals. Often these packages have the spices packaged separately, so parents can decide how much spice to add to the meal. The freeze-drying process is a little more extensive, so there is a price difference, but freeze-dried foods tend to have a longer shelf life than do dried foods.

Menu planning

When menu planning for canoe camping trips, we make a chart that blocks out the number of days on one axis and all the meals (including morning and afternoon snacks) on the other axis.

MENU PLANNER					
	Breakfast	Snack	Lunch	Snack	Supper
Day One					
Day Two					
Day Three					

Breakfast

Breakfast is often the easiest meal to plan. There are a variety of cooked cereals to choose from. These are generally high in fiber and seem to keep you feeling satisfied longer than ready-to-eat cereals. Adding dried fruits as the cereal is cooking improves its nutritional value and makes it more visually appealing by adding some color. Stirring milk powder into cooked hot cereal is a way of adding milk to the meal. It also results in a creamier cooked cereal.

Ready-to-eat cereals are relatively bulky if you have to bring enough for the whole family. However, they are great to have along as snacks for the kids. Handfuls of Cheerios or Shreddies mixed with dried fruit and nuts and packaged in individual resealable plastic bags are a popular and nutritious way to provide snacks.

Other traditional breakfasts include French toast and pancakes. To transport eggs for French toast or even scrambled eggs, use the carton they came in. This is designed to provide each egg protection. Cut the carton into the size needed and fit this into a plastic food storage container with a snap-on lid. Never crack open the eggs at home and transport them without their shells. Once an eggshell is cracked, salmonella bacteria (a common type of food poisoning found in poultry products) starts to multiply. If French toast is to be served later on a trip, powdered whole-egg products can be used. These are available at some of the larger outdoor stores.

Bread often gets squashed just going from the bakery to the cupboard, so it is hard to imagine taking fresh bread on a canoe trip. Get the children to count out the number of slices of bread that will be needed and have them put a slightly larger square of waxpaper between each slice. Put the alternating bread and waxpaper layers back into the bread bag and have the kids sit on it! Squash the bread so that it is as flat as it can get. Kids love this! The waxpaper makes it easy to separate the squashed bread slices later and this loaf is much easier to pack. When it comes time to make the French toast, simply soak the slices in the egg mixture a little longer than normal and they'll return to almost normal size.

Maple syrup can be heavy, bulky and make a sticky mess. Fake maple syrup eliminates these problems. When all the moisture is evaporated from real maple syrup, it turns into a candy sugar. Use the opposite principle to make fake maple syrup. Add a generous amount of brown sugar to a small amount of boiling water and stir this on the stove. The longer the sugar water is boiled, the thicker it becomes. When the mixture is ready to serve, add a few drops of maple flavoring. The consistency of the syrup may not be the same as the syrup used at home, but it sure tastes good.

Pancakes and camping seem to go hand in hand. Whether you make up your own mix using powdered eggs or you purchase the commercially available preparation, mixing them is easy for kids using the "shake, shake, shake" method. All you need is a sturdy large resealable plastic bag. Freezer bags are the most durable. Pour in the dry ingredients followed by the liquid ingredients, seal the bag and let the kids shake. Keep shaking until the batter is smooth and bubbly. Before handing the batter bag to a child, ensure that the bag is closed securely. Wearing pancake batter early in the morning is not really a fun way for young campers to start the day.

Pancakes options are limitless. Dried fruits can be soaked, reconstituted, and added to the pancake batter. Adding oatmeal, bran or wheat germ will increase their nutrient and fiber content. For a "heavier" pancake that will keep you feeling full longer, we add grated potatoes or potato flakes to the batter. We serve these potato pancakes with applesauce rather than syrup.

Applesauce is easy to pack if it is made into fruit leather. Fruit leathers are easy to make at home. Stew the fruit until it is softened, then pour it into the blender or food processor and puree. Pour the pureed fruit onto a non-stick baking sheet. Level it so that it is about ¼ inch thick and put it into the oven at 180F. Leave the door ajar about an inch. This allows the moisture and excess heat to escape so the fruit is dried not cooked. If your toddler or preschooler is helping you making the fruit leather, it is probably wise not to put it into the oven until after their bedtime, when it is safe to leave the oven door ajar. It will take several hours for the applesauce to dry, and when it's done it will have a candied, translucent look. After the pans come out of the oven, it is important to remove the dried fruit leather immediately or it may stick. Let the fruit leather cool on a cooling rack, then cut it into convenient-sized pieces and wrap it in plastic wrap. The most difficult part is keeping the kids out of it until the camping trip.

Granola is a breakfast favorite around many camping circles. It is simple and fast, may be eaten either hot or cold and is highly nutritious.

Homemade granola has the added bonus of allowing parents to control the sweetness and the fat content. Granola can be made easily in a skillet on top of the stove or in the microwave. Measurements and lists of ingredients for granola are just guidelines; you can vary what you put into the granola to suit your family's tastes.

Later in the day, granola can be used to make easy toppings for desserts such as apple crisps. One tablespoon each of flour and margarine transforms a cup of granola into a dessert topping. And, of course, granola and GORP (Good Old Raisins and Peanuts) mixed together makes a great midmorning snack.

Lunch

Lunches shouldn't take a lot of time to prepare. For us, they often consist of soups and sandwiches, with dried fruits for dessert.

There are lots of great dried soups available in grocery stores. Packages of single-serving soups give families the opportunity to mix and match. This gives the kids some choice and may encourage the more fussy eaters to finish their soup. Larger soup packages are available for one-pot soups. It's a good idea to take a look at the recommended cooking time before selecting a soup to take along on a trip. Some types take more time than others to prepare.

Be creative when it comes to soup. No one says you have to eat the soups just the way they are packaged. Adding instant rice or instant noodles to vegetable or tomato soup gives the soup more substance. Vegetable flakes can also be added for more variety. On cold rainy afternoons soup is a comfort food, while it also helps replenish fluids lost during the day.

With some supervision, your youngster can help make lunch. The more involved they are, the more likely they will be interested in eating the food.

Fillings for sandwiches are more limited while camping than they are at home because of the lack of cool storage. A little imagination can overcome this restriction and produce some interesting lunches that also keep well. On short weekend trips, fresh vegetables can be toted along. A crisp cucumber sandwich tastes great when you're sitting on the warm rocks watching the reflections in the lake. From peanut butter, to date spreads, to a wide variety of cheeses, sandwich fillings can be quite nutritious. In areas where cans are permitted, a small can of tuna, salmon or ham can be the "old reliable." One small can will make lunches for a family or four. When selecting cheeses to take along, it's important to check the moisture content, because cheese with more moisture is likely to go moldy faster. Packaged cheese slices, usually a favorite with kids, are a good choice for later in the trip. Because these packages do not require refrigeration until the package is opened, they can last indefinitely.

There are lots of possibilities for sandwich breads or crackers. The difficulty is in selecting ones that will travel well. Some denser breads, such as malt, pumpernickel or rye, pack well and last longer than airier sandwich breads. Bagels travel well but seem to mold faster than pita breads, so they should be eaten within the first few days of the trip. Plain tortilla breads last the longest. We have had grilled tortilla cheese sandwiches at the end of a month-long canoe trip!

Dinner

Dried meats such as beef or chicken jerky can be part of lunch, dinner or a snack. As part of dinner, they can be cut into little squares and added to one-pot meals or rehydrated in a powder-based gravy mix and served as roast beef for the traditional Sunday dinner.

For some reason, kids young and old seem to enjoy macaroni and cheese. Adding some rehydrated vegetables and chunks of jerky to the macaroni while it is cooking completes the nutritional requirements and makes a meal that is ready in under twenty minutes.

When planning dinners, try to think in terms of bases and sauces. The bases are the carbohydrate-rich foods that give you energy and fill you up. These include potatoes, rice, and pastas. The sauces can be vegetable and protein based. Meat alternatives such as kidney beans, or soybeans or chickpeas are excellent sources of protein, especially when combined with grains such as rice or pasta.

Bases tend to fall into two categories, instant or slow. Rice for example is available in the instant five-minute variety as well as a brown variety that takes forty-five minutes to cook. Parboiled rice takes about thirty-five minutes.

Potatoes also are available in many forms. For canoe trips that require little portaging, bringing fresh potatoes along is not a problem, but they do require more time to cook. Potato flakes and dried potato slices or cubes cook faster. Dried potato flakes can be used to thicken sauces if too much water was added by accident. This becomes more likely as young, inexperienced cooks begin to help out.

Pastas are an all-time favorite. The various shapes and sizes are a parents' dream because meals can take on lots of different looks and can be topped with many kinds of sauces. Common cheese or tomato sauces can be great places to hide nutritious vegetables. For example, crumbling dried spinach into tomato sauces hides the flavor and adds nutrients. Adding vegetables wherever possible improves your daily nutrition.

Tomato sauces are available in dried form, but making your own is simple to do. Tomato sauce can be dried in the oven using the same process as that used to make fruit leather. It is easiest to start with tomato paste. Spices can be added before the drying process or when the tomato leather is being rehydrated.

White sauces made with milk powder and thickened with flour can provide a wide variety of options. Add a little Parmesan cheese and garlic to the white sauce and you've got an Alfredo sauce. Or add cheddar. Regardless what you choose, this type of sauce is an excellent source of calcium. Adding a little extra milk powder doesn't influence the sauce but does increase the nutrient content. Adding vegetables to white sauces adds not only nutrients but also color.

Many people use hamburger in their one-pot meals at home. Unfortunately, taking any fresh or frozen meat on a camping trip is not a good idea. A safe substitute is textured vegetable protein (TVP). This is a soybean product that even looks like ground meat. When added to sauces with some beef-flavored bouillon, TVP looks and tastes like ground beef, but without the storage problems. TVP is available at many health food stores and at most bulk food stores. It is relatively inexpensive source of protein.

Packing tricks

For day trips, meals can simply be packaged together in a daypack with a thermos of hot beverage for cooler days or a large jug of water or some juice boxes for warm summer days. Packing along a water filter as well is a good idea. It doesn't take up much space and can provide you with all the fresh water that you want.

Once you start taking overnight trips, a little more effort needs to be put toward packing. Over the years we have narrowed it down to two methods. For shorter trips, we use a technique we call "Meal in a Bag." For this method we use a lot of kitchen garbage bags or grocery store bags. We use a large permanent marker to write the names of all the meals, one meal per bag: Saturday Breakfast, Saturday Lunch, Sunday Breakfast, etc. For longer trips, write Breakfast Day 1, Breakfast Day 2, etc., until you have a bag for every meal. Put all the food and condiments necessary for the meal into the appropriate bag

When using the Meal in a Bag method there are a couple of options for packing beverages. Packing all the beverages together in one stuff sack allows access to the beverages all the time, but this leaves no control as to how much gets used each day. If you only have a limited quantity of juice crystals, it is easy to run out before the trip is over. Another option is to put only enough beverages for the entire day with each morning meal. (This means remembering to pack the sugar packages and creamer for morning coffee in each Breakfast meal bag.)

The child's midmorning snack should be packed with the breakfast meal. This way there is less rummaging around in the pack. Remember to pack the meals in reverse order. If you are out for a five-day trip, then Day 5 meals will be at the bottom of the pack.

Another packing method is "Meals a la Carte." Rather than packing each breakfast separately, all the breakfasts are packaged together. All the lunches go in a separate bag, and all the dinners in another bag. With this method you pack condiments in large quantities. In the breakfast bag, for example, pack a larger bag of brown sugar that can be used to make the syrups for all the days when pancakes or hot cereal are on the menu. Rationing of condiments is important when using this method. The advantage to using Meals a la Carte is the flexibility of the meals. If it is raining on the day that pancakes were originally scheduled, it is easy to substitute granola from another day's menu. The only drawback is that least favorite meals may be left to the end of the trip.

Regardless of the method that you use to pack the meals, it is important to pack some "extras." This should include a few hearty dried soups, some instant potato flakes, some beef jerky, a few packages of instant oatmeal, etc. These should be packed at the bottom of the food pack and reserved for emergencies.

Cooking methods

Preparing meals in pots over a camp stove is virtually the same as cooking at home except the number of pots are restricted and foods need to be stirred more frequently.

Using a fire to cook can be done in several ways. Dingle-pole cooking is where a pot is dangled or suspended above the fire by a pole placed through the pot handle or from a chain hanging from a pole. This method is handy if there are no fire grates to set a pot on. One advantage of dingle-pole cooking is the ability to easily change the height of the pot and therefore adjust the temperature.

Putting a grate or fire bars on the rocks around the fire pit makes it easy to put the pot directly above the flame. Whenever the pot is directly on the fire, constant stirring is required to prevent the bottom from burning. It is hard to change the height of the grate or bars, so the heat is adjusted by adding small sticks to the fire as necessary. Allow children to locate sticks and hand them to an adult to put into the fire.

Another method is foil cooking. Food is wrapped in two layers of tinfoil and sealed as well as possible. The foil packages are then placed on a wire rack directly above on the warm bed of coals. Without any fuss, the food steams itself to perfection and is soon ready to eat. Some popular camp classics are prepared this way. Chocolate chips and marshmallows sandwiched between two graham crackers create "S'mores" (as in, "I want 'some more'"), a hit with most kids.

Cooking on a stick is not restricted to marshmallows. Bannock, a popular native bread, can be cooked in this manner. The batter is quite similar to biscuit batter. Whether you make up your own biscuit mix or you purchase a ready-made mix, simply add water and stir until the batter is dough-like. Little cooks may need some help turning their bannock regularly. Once it is golden brown it is ready to eat, but let the bannock cool slightly before removing it from the stick. It can be eaten plain, or let your imagination run wild. Fill the hole with peanut butter and jam, or roll a cheese slice up and let it melt in the hole.

Methods of baking over the fire or stove have evolved dramatically from the earthen ovens of the past. There are two types of reflector ovens. One uses heat generated by the sun, and another uses heat from a fire. Both work on the same principle. Heat is focused onto a baking surface by reflective panels set at precise angles. Baking with the aid of fire is efficient, and solar reflectors aren't practical for most camping trips, so your choice is fairly clear. With a properly maintained fire, a cake can be baked outdoors in the same length of time as it takes to bake one at home. The optimum fire pit is a horseshoe of rocks just the width of the reflector oven and about the same height. Sticks leaned up against the back of the fire pit creates a tall but small fire, ideal for reflector oven cooking. Because the heat is most intense at the front of the reflector oven, it's important to turn the food a quarter rotation at regular intervals to ensure all parts cook evenly.

Pizza is one of our more popular baked foods. Build the pizza by starting with yeast bread crust and adding layers of ingredients topped with a layer of cheese. Sausages that don't require refrigeration are a popular item, but we've also used freshly caught fish that has been filleted and sliced into cubes. The whole family can't wait until the pizza comes out of the reflector oven. While the first one is baking, everyone can work on building a second pizza, because it is so good that one is never enough.

Cakes, muffins and biscuits can be cooked on a reflector oven, but they also work well on an "Outback oven" on top of the camp stove. This is a covered non-stick frying pan that has a special asbestos-cloth-type cover that comes down over the sides of the pan to direct heat evenly around the pan and out through the vent at the top. They even come with a very simple temperature gauge that's calibrated to "warm, bake or burn." This is a modern version of Dutch oven cooking.

Gentle warning

Adults often wipe their hands on their clothes while cooking, and children sometimes spill food on their clothes while eating. It's important to rinse the smells out of clothing before retiring for the night, to avoid attracting animals.

Camping trips are a great opportunity to pass on skills to the younger generation. Children should feel like they are contributing in campsite activities.

Chapter 5

Developing Camp Skills

GOING CAMPING IS A GREAT OPPORTUNITY FOR PARENTS TO PASS on skills and knowledge to their children. There is a lot that children can learn about science, nature, being independent and getting along with other people when out in the wilderness.

Planning a trip

A successful trip begins at home, taking the time to go over maps and checking sources of information to plan a trip that is both manageable and interesting. Traveling downstream is always faster than going back up, so it's important to know which way a river flows when planning a route. If the trip is mostly on lakes or covers a circular route, it may not make much difference which direction is chosen. If the trip means traveling up and down the same stretch of river, it is smarter to start at the end of the river and paddle upstream. Going downstream first gives a false sense of ease that might entice a paddler to go farther than they should.

The first trips should always be fairly close to home, especially when young children are involved. That way if a problem crops up or the youngsters get homesick, it's easy to turn around and go back home. It's usually easy to find good ideas for short excursions close to home from local sources of information. Try phoning conservation areas, parks or talking to naturalists or canoe clubs for suggestions.

Many conservation areas and parks produce excellent maps with detailed canoe routes on them. These usually provide phone numbers to call and many offer good suggestions about the routes marked on the maps. Some even provide useful camping tips and highlight natural and historic points of interest. Tagging along with more experienced friends or going on trips organized by clubs are other good ways to ease into the process of planning your own trips.

Maps and compasses

Having good maps and knowing how to use them is an important skill. This was never more obvious to us than on a trip we took before we had kids. We'd set up a campsite on Rockaway Lake, on the Wildcat Loop in the southwest corner of Algonquin Park. We visited the huge white pines that still stand on a small piece of virgin forest, then portaged our canoe across to the next lake. Once there, we noticed another canoe of explorers. The rental canoe was paddled by a father and his ten-year-old son. It turned out that they weren't exploring the lake, they were trying to find the portage. They had a poor-quality map that looked like it had been produced from a photocopy several generations removed from the original. It was hard to make out details on the map and some of the information was out of date. They were already a day overdue and had at least another day's travel to get back to their car.

We guided them to the portage and gave the father some suggestions on how to carry his canoe more easily. He admitted that he was late because he was having such a hard time carrying the canoe over the portages. It was near suppertime by the time we returned to our campsite. We were just enjoying our meal when the father and son paddled up to our island and asked us to suggest possible campsites and to point out the portage out of the lake.

Later, as we were cleaning up our dishes, we noticed that their tent was set up, but their canoe was again headed back to our island. Might we have any food that we could spare, as their supplies were down to a few remaining scraps?

Before we left the lake the next morning, we paddled over and drew a little map for them outlining the route back to their car. Once they got to the end of the portage, they'd be paddling on lakes with cottages, so they'd be able to stop and ask directions.

When we got back to our car, we checked at the rental shop and were relieved to find that the father and son had made it back okay. But as we continued our journey, we wondered aloud what effect this outing would have on their relationship. Would the son lose respect for his father, or would the misadventure form a bond that they would share over the years?

Knowing how to use a compass isn't that important on a canoe route as long as you always travel with good maps and you're confident in your ability to read them. Lakes and rivers are always prominently marked, and as long as you don't get adventuresome and paddle at night or in a dense fog, you'll always be able to look on the map to see where you are. As long as you can see where you're going and can keep track of your progress, the compass shouldn't be necessary.

Topographic maps are usually the best kind to bring on a canoe trip, unless there is a good canoe route map available. "Topo maps," as they are often called, are available in a variety of scales that either give a good overview of the area on a single map or give you greater detail spread out over several maps. For most trips, the 1:50,000 scale maps are the best.

The key to using a map is to start by orienting the map to your surroundings, then pay attention to the landmarks as you travel along. As long as you're sure of the location you started from and you keep track of where you are as you travel, you won't get lost. The distinctive shape of the shoreline usually makes it fairly easy to follow your progress on the map. Keep the map in front of you on the bottom of the canoe and have it lined up with the direction you're traveling, even if that means the writing is upside-down. If you're concerned that you might lose track of your location if you take a break from paddling, mark it on the map in pencil so that you can find your location again when you get back in the canoe.

Being able to use a compass well can extend your trip by letting you do some bushwhacking to find little lakes or areas of interest further from the shoreline. The fastest and easiest way to learn how to use a compass is to take a course. It's not hard to learn when you've been shown how, but some of the finer points are a little hard to grasp without good explanation and practice.

In this electronic age, another navigation tool that's becoming afford-able for most people is a Global Positioning System (GPS) device. A GPS is a pocket-sized electronic receiver that locks onto the signal from satellites orbiting the earth. This gives the user an extremely accurate reference of where they are in terms of latitude and longitude. GPSs can be used to "remember" a route, and if you decide to venture into the bush to find that hidden fishing pond, the GPS can be used to guide you back to where you left the canoe. This system is much easier and more accurate than a compass, but even if you do use a GPS, it's still a good idea to bring along and know how to use a compass. The compass will always work, even when the batteries in your GPS have died.

Weather prediction

Traveling in the wilderness puts us at the mercy of the weather and it's important to have an understanding of what's coming our way in order to prepare ourselves.

Weather observation is a great activity to share with children. They can learn a lot of science from watching the weather, but it's equally important to just lie on your back with your kids beside you and watch the clouds to find imaginary shapes.

Predicting weather can be quite scientific, but there is a lot of folk-lore about weather that can be quite helpful in understanding what's going to happen, and children seem to enjoy learning through stories.

■ *Rhymes that reason*

The age-old rhyme, *Red sky at night, sailor's delight / Red sky in the morning, sailor take warning* is a good tool for predicting weather. The color in the sky at sunrise and sunset is caused by the low angle of the sun shining through the atmosphere. When the atmosphere is clear, the color of the light tends to be yellowish, but when the atmosphere contains a lot of particles, the color of the light becomes redder. During the day, heat from the sun evaporates water, which gradually rises into the atmosphere as vapor. As the vapor rises, it eventually encounters air that is cooler, where the vapor will condense as it comes in contact with airborne dust particles. When the sun begins to set, the suspended droplets of water often produce sunsets that range from brilliant red to subtle shades of pink. This test works best away from cities, as they may generate enough airborne particles that a red sky happens in spite of what the weather is going to do.

Overnight, the atmosphere cools, which causes the water vapor in the air to gradually drop back down to the ground. In the morning,

Because of their smaller body mass, children are more affected by weather than adults. On this trip to James Bay on the Missinabi, we learned the hard way how important good raingear is when the gear we brought started to fail.

the air will be clear again and the sunrise will be yellowish in color. The water vapor from the previous day's heat can often be found as dew on the grass and mist in the valleys. Dew or dampness on the grass first thing in the morning is a good sign that there won't be any rain during the day. A rhyme that helps us remember this is:

When the grass is dry in the morning light, look for rain before the night;
When the dew is on the morning grass, rain will never come to pass.

A pink sky in the morning means the moisture is still high in the air and will come down later as rain.

■ Wind signals

The direction of the wind is another good indicator of changing weather. When the weather is stable, the wind tends to come from a constant direction. We call this the prevailing wind. Where we live, the wind almost always comes from the west. If the wind swings around to the east, we know to batten down the hatches because rain is on the way. In fact, there's a rhyme that hints at the kind of weather to expect from an east wind: "When the rain is from the east, it is four and twenty hours at least." It's safe to assume that any rain that's accompanied by an east wind will be around for at least a day. Another direction rhyme that helps recall which wind direction indicates good or bad weather is:

> When the wind is from the west, it brings us the weather we like best;
> When the wind is from the east, it brings us the weather we like the least.

■ Mare's tails and sundogs

There are two basic kinds of mechanisms that can produce weather that we'd describe as bad. Large areas of weather move in air masses called fronts. A high-pressure area produces clear skies and pleasant weather. There is little humidity in the air and the temperatures are usually cool. A low-pressure area produces overcast skies and rain. Low pressure is usually accompanied by warm, moist air. Weather that's produced by most fronts takes quite a while to move in and out. When it starts to drizzle, it may take several days before the weather clears out again. The first hints that a front is moving in are the mare's tails clouds or sundogs.

Sundogs are caused by light passing through ice crystals that act like prisms. Before sundogs are visible, it is common to see long, thin, wispy clouds high in a clear, blue sky. These are often called "mare's tails" because they look much like the tail of a horse. After seeing the mare's tails, a haze will normally form in the sky. Depending on the time of day, there may be a halo or foggy ring around the sun (or moon), while at other times rainbow-like areas of color may be visible on either side of sun. These are called sundogs and they are a fairly reliable indication that rain can be expected within a day.

Weather travels at a fairly constant pace. Paying attention to the amount of time it takes between sighting mare's tails and when the sundogs become visible gives an indication of how fast the rainy weather is traveling. The weather system can be broken down into thirds: one third for it to arrive, one third while it hangs around, and one third for it to clear up. The amount of time it takes for the sky to become quite gray will be similar to the amount of time that it will probably be raining or drizzling. Once the precipitation starts to lessen, it will take about the same amount of time for it to clear out as it took to go from the first mare's tail clouds to the beginning of the rain. As with most things relating to weather, this is only a rough guideline.

■ *Thunderstorms*

The other way that weather is produced is by the heat and humidity generated from the sun. This often results in violent winds and torrential rain, but it usually only lasts for a short time. The danger in thunderstorms is that they can develop quickly and give campers only a short time to take shelter. Weather that produces severe thunderstorms can often appear to be almost the same weather that seemed to be perfect the day before.

Days that will produce thunderstorms usually begin hot and humid. There will be puffy white clouds that are large and high in the sky early in the morning. By afternoon, they'll become towering columns of clouds with billowing masses that indicate internal turbulence. If there is lots of vertical movement of air inside the clouds, large amounts of water will be taken high up, where it will suddenly come in contact with cool air in the upper atmosphere. When that happens, the moisture will suddenly condense into ice and start to fall back to the ground again. With luck, the heat of the day will melt the ice into large amounts of rain by the time it comes back to earth. If not, it comes down as hail.

This aggressive movement of air often generates a lot of lightning activity and high winds.

Strong wind and heavy rain from these clouds can come quickly. Rather than being one big storm, this type of weather is made up of a series of localized storms that build and dissipate quickly. The dangerous cloud masses are the ones that are tall and billowing. Generally clouds that have an anvil shape at the top are losing their strength and are not a cause for concern. Individually, these localized storms often don't last more than an hour. However, the series of thunderstorms may continue to form for many hours. A rhyme that children may use to remember how to predict this kind of weather system is:

When clouds make castles up to the sky,
Thunder will rumble and lightning will fly.

■ *Animal forecasters*

Clouds aren't the only things that can help us predict weather. Many people look to animals to provide hints as to what the weather will do next.

One example: Folklore has it that when the swallows are flying low, it'll probably rain; if the swallows are flying high, the weather will be clear. The rhyme for this is:

When the swallows fly high, the sun will be in the sky;
When the swallows fly low, rain has not far to go.

There are good reasons why this works out in practice. In the humid air that often precedes periods of rain, flying insects usually stick fairly close to the ground, and that's where the swallows zoom in and out scoop them up. On days that promise good weather, the air will be cool and there will be little humidity. The heat from the sun will cause the air to rise, and insects are more likely to be lifted higher in the sky by the wind. Since swallows are insect-eaters, they will be flying where their supper is.

■ *Weather math*

A fun thing to do with kids is to use the chirps of crickets to calculate temperatures. Using an accurate watch, count the number of chirps in fifteen seconds and add thirty-seven to get an approximate Fahrenheit temperature.

Children often get quite frightened in thunderstorms. It helps to calm them if you can give them an idea of how far away a thunderstorm really is. Get them to watch for the flash of lightning and count the number of seconds before they hear the thunder. Thunder will travel about one mile for every five seconds (one kilometer for every three seconds). If you have a map nearby, you can show them where they are, point out a few features off in the distance and show them how much farther away the storm is than the things they can see.

■ *Using fires*

Campfires add a magical element to camping trips and a lot of people just don't feel like they've been in the wilderness unless they've enjoyed at least one campfire along the way. There is quite a bit of skill involved in being able to reliably get a fire started under any circumstance. It was important to us that our children learn how to safely start and manage campfires when they got older.

■ Selecting wood

Gathering good firewood is a greatly underrated skill. In order for wood to burn well it needs to be carefully selected. It should come from dead wood that has had quite a bit of time to dry. Wood that is starting to rot will weigh more and break apart more easily because it has absorbed moisture. Choose hardwood for fires whenever possible, as there are fewer sparks, which makes it safer for children. Don't use wood from live trees.

It's important to gather wood in a way that doesn't harm the environment or leave obvious visual scars. Select only smaller pieces of dead wood that are easily broken or can be gathered without much effort. Avoid cutting with a saw or using an ax. By collecting only wood that is a couple of inches in diameter, it's unlikely that you'll disturb any nesting cavities or shelters used by animals. Try not to gather all your wood in one place. Leave some for other campers who may use the area after you've moved on.

While gathering wood, quiz your child to see if they can point in the direction of the canoe or campsite. This will help them develop a better sense of direction and will give you more confidence that they won't later wander off and become lost.

When it has been raining, it may be hard to find dry wood to get the fire started. One of the best things to keep in mind in this situation is that you can "go to the living to find the dead." Near the bottom of most live spruce or other coniferous trees, there will be sheltered branches that have died and not yet fallen off. These branches are usually well sheltered even from strong downpours. If the branches snap easily, they'll make great firestarter. If they seem to want to bend, they may not have been dead that long and should be left alone. It doesn't take long to find enough small wood to get a fire started even after several days of constant drizzle. Once a twig fire is burning well, firewood that may be damp can be put on top of the fire, where it will dry, then burn.

■ Sure fire

When constructing a fire, be sure that air can circulate around and through it to provide oxygen. Putting wood that's too large on the fire too soon will smother it. At the same time, it's also important to make sure that the circulating air doesn't get so strong that it blows the fire out. Building a horseshoe of rocks around the fire helps to cut down the wind.

A large sheet of mosquito netting doesn't take much space in a pack, but it's a priority item to take along on trips with children. It's a portable sanctuary from the bugs during nap time, play time or meals.

There are two basic structures used in building good fires: the teepee construction and the log cabin construction.

The teepee begins as a loose circle of sticks that rest on the ground at one end and form a tent-like structure over top of the tinder. Once the fire is underway, additional wood is no longer placed in the teepee structure but is laid horizontally on the fire. Teepee fires are easy to start, good for warming the hands, providing light, and for cooking with reflector ovens.

The log cabin structure looks like a miniature log foundation in which a box-like structure is built up around the tinder. Since flames rise, the log cabin structure isn't as easy to get started as the teepee construction, however it does have an advantage in strong winds. Log cabin structures are useful for most cooking fires.

When a fire starts to go out, or there's a sudden need for flames from a fire that's already burned down to coals, people often want to lean down and blow on the fire to get it started again. This can be a dangerous practice, as sparks from the fire can easily fly back and land in an eye. The safest way to get a fire going again is to use a hard, flat surface such as a plate or pot lid to fan the fire.

On every camping trip, there should be several packages of matches and lighters that are kept in different locations. Matches and lighters should be kept in waterproof containers. By keeping them stored separately, there is always a backup if a lighter stops working or package of matches gets lost or wet.

Pitching tarps for shelter

The process of getting a tarp properly set up can be a frustrating nightmare or a fun family project, the difference is in knowing a few simple tricks and doing a little planning. Setting up a tarp is a good idea at most campsites when traveling with children, because it provides shelter against sun, wind and rain. Putting up a tarp is generally much easier when there are lots of helping hands. Even young children can help by holding ropes while the tarp is adjusted.

Choosing the best location for a tarp requires some thought. Will the spot provide shelter once the tarp is up? Are there appropriate trees nearby for anchoring the tarp? Will the ropes that support the tarp get in the way of traffic and trip people? Often when people pitch tarps, they simply tie cords to all four corners and suspend it from trees nearby. This is usually acceptable for wind or sun, but the first time it rains, the water pools in the tarp and the extra weight often makes the whole thing collapse or rip open. The way to prevent this is to keep the center of the tarp from sagging. Rain will run off the tarp if the center of it forms a peak. The easiest way to get a peak in a tarp is to drape it over a rope that's been suspended quite high up between two trees, then anchor all four corners on the ground. This makes a bit of an "A" shape that sheds water and wind.

Another way to get a peaked roof is to attach a rope to the fabric somewhere near the center of the tarp and raise this up fairly high. When the corners are anchored to the ground or trees it will make a pyramid shape that easily sheds water and wind. To attach a rope in the center, place a small, smooth stone or pine cone in the middle of the tarp. Tie a strong cord tightly around the fabric with a knot that won't come undone to trap the stone and provide an anchor that won't damage the tarp. This allows you to raise the center of the tarp as high as you wish. Now all you need to do is find a high branch to toss the rope over and haul the center of the tarp up.

Any time you raise a tarp, it's best to first place the tarp about where you want it. Loosely tie off the outer edges with knots that can be easily untied and adjusted. Once you get the whole thing up, you can go around and adjust the tension on all the anchor points to get it exactly where you'd like it.

The backwoods biffy

For proper wilderness toilet etiquette, we recommend that you don't look to the animals and learn by example. At every campsite or stop along the way, all bathroom activities should take place well away from water sources. Many established campsites have an outdoor privy installed a short distance back in the bush. There's usually an obvious path to the privy, and it's important to take your children there and explain how to use it. Most backcountry outhouses consist of a box about chair height with a hole cut in the top and a lid to cover the hole.

If there is no established facility, one will have to be constructed. The location should offer some privacy, be away from the bugs, have at least six inches of soil, and be situated well away from water. It's also nice if there's a comfortable log to use as the toilet seat. Dig a small trench in the soil to catch solid matter. The goal is to dig an area that's just big enough to hide a small amount of solid human waste. If possible, try to remove any intact grass so it can be placed back over the trench to cover it up when everything is done. It's best if a trench is made in a new location for every use, that way it doesn't require a deep trench and it won't take as long to for the waste to decompose.

For really young children who are being toilet trained, it's a good idea to bring along a lightweight plastic toilet seat that can be supported on two branches or logs. At the toddler stage, many kids are just getting the hang of using a toilet, so it's important not to confuse them when they are out camping.

Toilet paper is biodegradable, so it will be absorbed back into nature, but it takes a long time to disappear. Finding piles of toilet paper lying about at the back of a campsite is a not a pleasant sight, so it's important to dispose of it properly. There are some parks in environmentally sensitive areas where it is mandatory to pack out all waste, including human excrement. Fortunately, most areas don't require campers to go to that extreme. Some campers bury their toilet paper, other campers prefer to bury only the waste and keep the toilet paper separate, to be burned in a fire later. Kids are often not good at dealing with used toilet paper. Check the toilet area occasionally.

When packing toilet paper for the camping trip, put individual rolls in re-sealable freezer bags to keep them waterproof. Keep one roll accessible in a location that everyone knows about and can easily get to. Keep the others tucked safely near the bottom of other packs. One helpful tip we use to keep the toilet paper dry is to remove the cardboard core from the center of the roll before putting it in the bag. Pulling the paper from the center of the roll means you don't have to take it out of the bag. Toilet paper is a fairly precious commodity on a camping trip and it's sad to see it unraveling down a hill because it got away when someone dropped a roll.

A good way to solve the problem of not wanting to go outside with the mosquitoes if there's a need to go "pee" during the night is to bring an empty jar into the tent to use as a chamber pot.

When traveling with young ladies who are just beginning menstruation, it is difficult to predict when they will be start their cycle, as young teens often have irregular cycles. Packing some sanitary napkins in the first-aid kit is always a good idea. These pads are designed to absorb blood, and as a result, they make excellent bandages for large wounds. Keeping a supply of "liners" and absorbent pads in the first-aid kit is great idea for first-aid as well as a precaution to accommodate unanticipated menstrual periods.

Feminine hygiene products shouldn't be buried. Put pads and tampons into a resealable plastic bag, then burn them at the end of the day. They should always be burned, because the smell of blood may be attractive to some animals.

There may be occasions when these need to be carried out due to bans on the use of fires. If a fire ban exists, keep used sanitary napkins, tampons and diapers away from animals by packaging them in a strong re-sealable waterproof bag and hanging that up between trees in a manner similar to hanging the food packs. When kept this way, they can be brought out for proper disposal at the end of the trip.

All garbage must be either packed out or burned. Nothing should be left behind when you leave a campsite, even if that means packing out someone else's garbage. Many items of garbage can be burned safely if a fire is being used. Tents should always be located upwind of fires.

Grime isn't a crime

Staying clean on a camping trip requires that campers use several different types of cleaning supplies. Choose soaps and detergents that have the least impact on the environment. Look for the terms phosphate-free and biodegradable on the label. When using them, keep them away from the main water supply. Bring some type of wash basin along to allow you to carry any dirty water back into the bush, well away from the river or lake. When it is disposed of in the soil, plants will absorb it. We put all cleaning supplies into a small wash basin, then put that in the pack we use for our kitchen gear. This helps to keep these supplies together and adds only minimal extra weight.

On weekend camping trips, dirty laundry can simply be kept separate and cleaned at home; dishes and personal hygiene are the main concerns. Longer camping trips will require that some laundry be done along the way.

Biodegradable soaps are available in both liquid and bar forms. For camping trips, the bar forms are more convenient. Sunlight laundry bar soaps are phosphate-free and the surfactant is biodegradable. Surfactants are the ingredients that reduce the surface tension of water, helping it to penetrate deeply into the fabric. This encourages the dirt to be released into the water as the clothing is agitated in the wash basin. The surfactants then help to keep the dirt suspended in the wash water so that they do not settle back into the clothing.

For washing the body, a bar soap that will float on the surface of the water is handy. Ivory soap will float because there are little air bubbles whipped into it.

Dishwashing liquids are designed to remove grease. Small quantities of this liquid can be brought along in well-sealed, waterproof containers. Not only can it be used to keep dishes clean, but a small drop of dishwashing liquid can also be used to shampoo hair.

Soaps are made with some type of fatty substance as the base. This is something that animals find attractive. Bars of soap should be kept out of reach with the food pack overnight. One of our friends told us about a grizzly bear that wandered through their camp and ignored freshly baked muffins, but took great delight in a bar of soap.

The main objective of dishwashing is not only to remove the remaining food particles, but also to make the dishes free from bacteria or germs. The best way to do this is with a three-step method: remove the food by cleaning in dish washing liquid and hot water; briefly soak the dishes in a sanitizing solution (see below); then remove any traces of soaps or sanitizers by thoroughly rinsing with hot water. When traveling with a group there are more people to carry the load, so taking three light, plastic wash basins should be no problem. This way basins can all be set in a row, and the dishes can simply be passed from one stage to the next. After the dishes have been washed, it is best to air dry them if possible. Nylon mesh stuff sacks are useful for this purpose.

The sanitizer for the rinse cycle at home or in restaurants is often bleach. While taking a small leak-proof bottle of liquid bleach in our packs is possible, bleach in powder form is preferable. Powdered bleaches that are chlorine- and phosphate-free are available at some grocery stores and in bulk food stores. As powdered forms of bleach are generally concentrated, only a pinch of bleach is necessary for any wash up. Ones that are made from sodium carbonate (washing soda) and hydrogen peroxide will decompose into oxygen, water and soda ash. To transport this powdered bleach, small waterproof containers (preferably ones with childproof lids) should be used. This bottle *must* be labeled clearly and kept out of the reach of the children.

Traveling on long canoe trips means that bathing and hair washing will need to be done. Certainly, a dip in the lake and a rub down with a washcloth and water will remove most of the surface dirt, but many people prefer to use a bit of soap. Anytime that soaps are used, wash water should be kept well away from water sources. Warming up a large pot of water to be scooped cup by cup onto hair seems to work well. If the person leans over a wash basin, the soapy water can be contained. Sponge baths either in the tent or out in the open offer a cleansing option for adults and children alike. Young children and infants are probably best washed in the shelter of the tent, as cool breezes may give them a chill.

Most kids have a natural fascination with wild animals. The trick for parents is balancing the opportunity to learn with the need to keep both the children and the animals safe.

Chapter 6

. . . .

Wildlife

ONE OF THE MAJOR ATTRACTIONS THAT BRINGS FAMILIES TO THE wilderness is the chance to encounter animals in their natural environment. Helping children develop a respect for these animals and their environment is essential. Just as you teach a child that they cannot simply walk up to any dog and pet it, children need to know that wild animals are *wild* and they need their own space. In a zoo, signs remind visitors not to feed the wildlife and not to cross into the animal's boundaries. While there are no such signs in the wilderness, the same principles apply. "People food" should never be offered to animals.

Children are naturally curious about animals. Just as they are drawn to animal shows on television, they can also be drawn to animals in the wild. In North America, average-sized adults are big enough that they have little to fear from most large predatory animals, but small children can become a target. It is important to keep kids close to the adults when traveling in areas that might be a problem.

We wanted our children to learn that they should ask before approaching animals, both for their own sake and for the sake of the animals. Wild animals need to know that the humans that are in their environment are not a threat to them. One way of doing this is to always make sure the animal has an escape route before you approach. Knowing which mammals, birds and reptiles are indigenous to the area is important. When you are traveling in grizzly country, you need to know ahead of time what to do to be prepared for an encounter. When you are tripping in rattlesnake country, you should know what a rattler looks like and where they are normally found. Not understanding what time of year that bull moose are likely to behave aggressively can have serious consequences. Do some basic researching on the habitat, food supply and behavior of animals that you may encounter. Remember that we are only visitors in their home. If we do not do them any harm, then they will probably not do us any harm.

There are many sources for good information on animals and their behaviors. Interpretative staff for wilderness parks and conservation areas can often provide a wealth of information on the plant and animal life in their areas. They may also be able to tell you where interesting animals have been sighted and what time of day you might expect find them there. Knowing the eating habits of resident wildlife will also help point you in the right direction for seeing them in their natural environment. Local libraries and bookstores usually stock interpretive guidebooks that describe specific animal habitats and provide information on their behavior.

It is also important to know how a given animal demonstrates uneasiness and aggression before seeking it out in the wild. Some of these behaviors may be misinterpreted and put you and your family in danger unless you have done your research. Humans can be unwittingly disruptive, especially when they encounter young animals. Unusual behavior in an animal may be the result of a mother trying to distract you from her young. In the springtime, it's important to be aware of the possibility that your presence may be perceived as putting young animals at risk. You should always be prepared to back away and leave the animals in peace. Animals are generally as afraid of you as you are of them. Demonstrate respect.

Children are naturally inquisitive, and parents need to be prepared to answer questions and guide their children into being curious enough to learn more. We've always tried to help our children learn as much as possible from their animal encounters. We often retell the stories of some of our more memorable encounters as they grow older. They enjoy the stories, but even more important, as they grow older they become better able to understand what happened during the encounters they had when they were younger.

Animals fascinate most children, but it's hard to keep kids quiet enough to get close. We took lots of time approaching this muskrat in the Tiny Marsh and were able to get close enough to watch him eat breakfast.

The dilemma

There is no supermarket in the wilderness. In order to survive, an animal is either a hunter, or they are hunted. People don't spend a lot of time in the wilderness, so few witness the life-and-death struggle that goes on every day. As parents, we need to be prepared to help our children understand the predator–prey relationship in the wild.

When Kyle was six years old and Brendan was three, we took a November canoe trip to Tom Thomson Lake in Algonquin Park, Ontario. On this trip, we witnessed one of nature's life-and-death struggles from a front-row seat. It had been a cold, blustery weekend and we were hard-pressed to find a campsite that would let us get out of the sleet and snow. The trees in the forest had long since shed their leaves, and the wind sliced through the bare branches with little resistance. As we neared one of the designated campsites on a point of land that juts into the lake, we noticed a flurry of motion. As we got closer, it became apparent that a pine marten (a large member of the weasel family) was chasing a rabbit at full tilt. The rabbit frantically tried to shake its pursuer.

At first Kyle thought that he was watching the animals playing. Knowing that the chase could come to an end in the clearing, we explained to Kyle and his brother why the marten was chasing the rabbit. The kids had seen the outcomes of animal chases on TV, but we wanted to make sure they understood the reality they might witness. We tried not to portray the marten as the bad guy; he was simply trying to get a meal. We pointed out to the boys how cold it was and that hunting animals needed to eat lots at this time of year to be able to survive the winter. When it seemed clear that they favored neither animal as the winner, we paddled closer to get a better look.

The chase disappeared out of sight for what appeared to be the last time. We took the opportunity to paddle to shore so that we could get out of the canoes to stretch our legs and look around. Within a few minutes, we heard the rustle of leaves, and soon the rabbit was back with the marten in hot pursuit. We froze in our tracks, as we were afraid that our presence would have an impact on the chase. Either the rabbit might be startled and stop long enough that the marten would catch it, or the marten might notice us and give up the chase. Either way, we would have had consequences for the lives of the animals involved in the chase.

As it turned out, we needn't have worried. Our presence was completely ignored, and on one occasion both animals ran right over the feet of one of the spectators without seeming to notice them at all. Now that we were so much closer, the chase became more personal to us, and we could observe things that were not as apparent from a distance. Most remarkable was the marten's ability to follow the rabbit. from our human vantage point, we could watch where the rabbit was going, but the marten couldn't see its quarry because of obstructions in its path. The only way that the marten could know where the rabbit had gone was to follow its scent trail. It was amazing to see this being done with pinpoint precision at a dead run. It gave us a little insight into this animal's ability to perceive its world in a way that we can't even imagine.

Eventually the rabbit began to slow down, and it looked like the chase was almost over. In a final, desperate attempt to escape the danger, the rabbit ran down to the water near where the canoes were.

Then, with one last glance over its shoulder, it slipped quietly into the water and started swimming toward the opposite shore. Within moments, the marten was at the spot where the rabbit stepped off the shore, but it didn't notice the rabbit in the water. Instead, it ran in circles, trying to pick up the scent of the missing rabbit. Eventually, it started following the scent trail back in the direction it had come.

Though the rabbit had narrowly escaped the fangs and claws of the marten, it had perhaps exchanged a fast, violent death for a slow, peaceful one. Since it was near freeze-up time on the lakes, the rabbit was in great peril from the cold, because its fur was not designed to provide insulation in water. The numbing cold would soon rob the rabbit's strength, making it unlikely that the rabbit would reach the opposite shore without drowning.

We waited long enough to be sure that the marten could no longer find the rabbit, then our sympathies for the poor creature that had endured so much got the better of us. We quickly got into the canoes and headed out to rescue the swimmer. It took but a moment to catch up with the rabbit and scoop it into a canoe. It was exhausted and accepted its new fate with resignation, either understanding that we meant no harm or too exhausted to care. After toweling the wet, bedraggled rabbit off, we let Kyle bundle it up to keep it warm. We continued on our way, and after we were sure that the rabbit was warm and dry enough, we looked for a good place to set it back on shore.

As we set the rabbit down, we talked to the boys about the implication of what we'd just done. It was obvious that the rabbit would have died in the water if we hadn't rescued it. By saving the rabbit, we had meddled in nature's ways, and we explained that we should be careful about doing that. The new location that we gave the rabbit was as similar as we could manage to the place where we'd found it, but we pointed out to the boys that we might have unknowingly created a problem by putting the rabbit in another rabbit's territory.

Still, even after looking at what we had done as potentially wrong, we all had to admit that if felt good to have given the poor creature a second chance. As we paddled off, we wished it well.

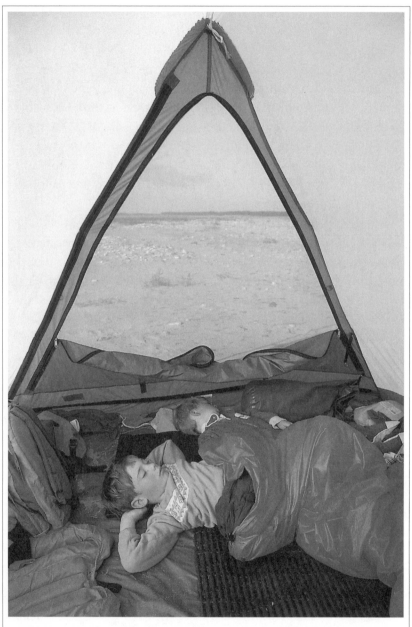

Finding perfect wilderness campsites is more challenging for families. This site on the lower sections of the Moose River near James Bay offered endless beaches.

Chapter 7

Campsite Selection

*A*s the last rays sunshine bathe the sky in shades of scarlet and orange, the silhouettes of wind-sculptured white pine conjure images of graceful Tai Chi postures. From somewhere on the other side of the mist, the haunting cry of the loon drifts across the mirror-smooth lake. A family rests in polished pockets of granite, absorbing the warmth that the rock has stored from the sun. As the light fades in the west, stars reveal themselves from horizon to horizon. Conversation is replaced by stifled yawns, and with some reluctance, the family retires to their cozy sleeping bags for a peaceful night's rest.

Choosing the perfect campsite is an acquired skill that's usually developed through the process of spending many nights in not-so-great places. Picking out good spots is as much an exercise in avoiding former mistakes as anything else. Selecting a nice site for adults can be a challenge, but choosing one that's also suitable for children is harder. There are some guidelines to keep in mind.

It helps to start the selection process if you have a good idea of what you're looking for in a campsite. Are you looking for a great view? A safe place for your kids to play? Do you want to be near animals? Are you expecting bad weather to roll in? Do you need to find a place with a breeze to keep the bugs at bay? How long do you plan to stay? Do you need to find a place that's out of the wind? Some of these goals work against each other, so you need to determine what's most important and look for campsites that meet your top priorities.

Things that go bump

No matter how well a trip is planned or how much experience you have, there will be occasions where you'll be forced to spend a night in places you didn't want to be. One memorable occasion when this happened to us was on Cross Corner Lake at the edge of Algonquin Park. We had miscalculated how long it would take to cover a few portages and now had to scramble to find an adequate campsite. We finally set up camp in among some tall poplars. A small spot just large enough to pitch a tent had been created along a bit of a trail. We made a quick supper on our stove and got ready for bed early so we could get a quick start the next day to make up the time we'd lost.

Just as we were finishing clean up, a pack of wolves began howling from somewhere across the lake. Not long afterwards, a second pack answered from somewhere behind us. We took some time to enjoy the serenade, then headed into the tent. We were rudely awoken in the middle of the night by the sound of many hooves passing on either side of the tent. We were directly in the path used by the area's moose to reach their preferred feeding spots. Unzipping the tent and shining a flashlight had identified the visitors, but it was hard to say who was most surprised.

It is important to check campsites for signs of animal life. Tracks in soft soil, scat in the bush, or marks on the trees can all indicate potential problems. We now think twice about pitching a tent in any area that looks like a path.

Bandits

If you camp in well-used areas you have to be careful with your food, as previous campers may have been careless with theirs. Animals in the area may be accustomed to looking for easy pickings around such campsites. Raccoons seem to be among the most well-versed in pilfering a camper's food supply. Suspending your food supply from a tree is one of the best ways to ensure that it will be there in the morning. Make sure the food pack is hung at least twice as far from any branches as you might think you have to put it. Raccoons are natural acrobats. On one trip we were awoken during the night by the sounds of animals squabbling. When we shined the flashlight up into the trees, where our food pack was hanging, we discovered two raccoons dangling precariously from a small branch overhanging the pack. Their combined weight bent the branch close enough to the pack that they were just able to reach it. They had already managed to unbuckle one strap and seemed intent on opening the other.

Mice, chipmunks and squirrels all have really sharp teeth that can cut a hole in a pack or tent in no time at all. It's important to keep this in mind, especially when camping in well-traveled areas. Before putting the food pack away for the night, it's a good idea to go through your children's clothes and belongings to check for food. It's not unusual for youngsters to stash snacks or candies in their pockets or their backpacks.

We always try to set up our kitchen area some distance from our sleeping area. If you place a tarp under the kitchen area, you can wash off any spills in the river or lake once the meal is over. Kids often drop things and it's much easier to notice a dropped morsel of food or piece of cutlery on the tarp than it would be to find it on the ground.

In the deep wilderness, bears are rarely a problem, but in more populated areas, some bears have learned to associate people with an easy meal. It isn't easy to predict what type of food will attract a bear. Some seem to have a sweet tooth, others may crave salty things, yet others seem intent on examining the entire food pack regardless of what's in it.

When we travel in areas where there may be a bear problem, we place our food either in large barrels or suspended in the food pack about six or seven feet off the ground. To give us some warning that we have a problem, we fasten our cooking pots on the outside of the food pack. That way, we'll hear the clanging of the pots if a bear starts nosing around, and we will have some time to consider our options. Avoid putting food between the tent and the canoes, just in case you have to beat a hasty retreat.

If there are scratches or claw marks at about eye level it may mean that a bear has chosen one of the trees as a signpost to mark his territory. Seeing a tree with this kind of marking should make you reconsider spending a night at this location, especially if the marks are fresh. Even if there are no signs of territorial marks on the trees, we usually examine campsites for fresh tracks to get an idea who's been visiting recently.

Forty days and forty nights

Drainage is often a problem in campsites. Examine the area where you plan to camp and study the slope where you'd like to put your tent. Is it in a low spot? Are there signs of runoff from previous rainstorms? Are there hills above the tent site that will gather and direct rainfall toward you? If you wind up in a sudden downpour, where will the water go?

Sandy areas provide good drainage, as the water is absorbed into the sand when it rains. Tent pegs don't hold well in the sand, but if there are any large rocks available, you can put one on top of each of the pegs to hold them in place. Make sure you know how many pegs you used and count them when you're packing away the tent. It's easy to lose pegs in the sand. One of the most difficult challenges when camped on sandy sites is keeping the sand out of the sleeping area. We try to have a tarp or mat outside the tent door to dust ourselves off before going in the tent.

Pitching a tent on a bed of moss may seem like a comfortable spot on warm, dry summer nights, but if it rains, the tent will be on top of a wet sponge. Even if it doesn't rain, dampness can seep up through the floor when the tent is pitched on moss. Pegs may not hold that well in moss either.

Pitching a tent in an area that's mostly rock is tricky because you can't drive in pegs. Most tents today are free-standing and don't require much in the way of pegs to set up, but they still need some support to ensure that the wind won't affect them and that the rain runs off properly. The easiest way of making sure the tent is stretched out properly and won't blow away is to use sticks instead of pegs and place rocks on the sticks to hold them in place. Rocks can be hard on tent bottoms, so you should try to keep a ground sheet underneath for extra protection. If you use a ground sheet, make sure that it doesn't extend beyond the tent floor. If it hangs over, tuck it underneath. In the event of rain, a ground sheet that extends beyond the floor will gather rain water and draw it under the tent, where it will create a puddle.

Rocky areas don't absorb much water and the runoff can be severe during strong downpours. In contrast, soil and sand can absorb a lot of rain before it starts to form pools and cause a runoff problem. Study the area where you're going to pitch the family tent and try to not pick a spot that will turn into a river during a thunderstorm.

Whenever you pitch a tent, it's a good idea to check the area underneath it to make sure there's nothing sticking up that might put a hole in the tent. To make sure the place you've chosen is suitable, it's a good idea to unroll the tent or the ground sheet in the spot where you plan to pitch it and have everyone in the family lie down in the place they'd like to spend the night. This gives you an opportunity to check for lumps and bumps before you've invested any time in setting it up.

Location is everything

We like camping on points of land or small islands because it's easier to keep a watch on the kids. Because of the terrain, they can't wander far and will always be visible. When we arrive at a campsite, we walk through the entire area with the kids and point out things that they need to watch out for. Poison ivy or poison oak patches are always one of our big concerns. If there's too much of it we'll move on before setting up the tent. If there is a small patch, we'll rope the area off or give instructions to not go near the area and tell them why.

Sometimes good campsites are located a little too high above the water to be really safe for children. A straight trip down to the water may cause a child to tumble. When our boys were younger, we always looked for zigzag pathways that they could manage more easily. We also taught them a little song that we made up about wiggle-waggling that they could sing every time they wanted to go down to the water. Rhymes, songs and fun chants are great ways to help the child to remember safety rules.

Ideal family campsites are attractive to parents and yet provide safe, fun places for kids. A perfect campsite should be free of bugs, sheltered from the wind, have no obstructions that hide children from sight, and should be situated beside clear, clean water. Shallow water for wading and a sandy beach are high priorities for kids. Campsites with cliff faces may be picturesque, but they present a safety hazard for youngsters. A great family spot provides as many opportunities for natural entertainment as possible, while at the same time minimizes safety hazards.

Tide in stride

If you wish to spend time paddling and camping along coastlines, keep in mind that beaches are devoid of vegetation for a good reason. When storms come up, they punish the shoreline, and putting a tent below the trees on the beach is an invitation for trouble if bad weather comes your way. Enjoy the beach, but try to put your tent in the trees. If you do opt for a beach site along an ocean, make sure you know where the high-tide mark is, thereby avoiding waking up in the middle of the night to find your gear floating away.

Tent on stilts

During the winter, we've often extended our paddling season by doing canoe trips in the Florida Everglades during the Christmas break. Camping in the Everglades is significantly different than what we've been accustomed to in the northern climates. Campsites along the coastline are on the beach or on some of the little offshore islands. In the interior, the National Park system has constructed elevated platforms, called Chickees, because there are few areas of solid ground on which to pitch a tent otherwise. Spending the night on Chickees takes a bit of getting used to. The platforms are not big, so it was quite easy to keep track of the kids, but we were concerned about losing some of cutlery and other small stuff. The chickees are made of wooden planks with gaps between them. Anything that fell between the cracks would be gone forever. We put a tarp across as much of the area as possible to catch anything that might fall.

It's important to be able to maintain a traveling schedule when camping in the interior regions of the Everglades. If you haven't allowed enough time to get to a campsite, you'll wind up sleeping in your canoe, as there will be no other choices available. The transition from day to night in the subtropics happens much faster than it does up north, so it's even more important to plan to be finished traveling at a reasonable hour in the afternoon.

Raccoons seem to be even more of a problem in the Everglades than they are in northern parks. Not only do you have to keep them out for your food, but they are also keenly interested in any fresh water you might have. There are more poisonous insects, animals and plants in southern climates than in the north, so there are new hazards to prepare for any time a trip is planned in the south. Doing your research will pay dividends. It's also a good idea to get advice from locals before heading into the backwoods. Most areas that offer back-country camping provide information at the registration office. Be sure to spend time with a park warden to learn as much as possible.

Our son Brendan was born near Christmas, so he's often been in strange locations on his birthday as we go traveling. One of his most memorable birthdays was spent on a Chickee in Hell's Bay in the Everglades. Just after sun up, we were getting his birthday breakfast ready and we noticed some ripples headed our direction through the water. Guessing what it might be, we quickly rousted the boys out of the tent. Just as they were rubbing the sleep out of their eyes, a manatee swam past us, lingering a bit out of curiosity. After breakfast, we watched from the platform as medium-sized nurse shark swim by. Brendan was ecstatic.

No-trace camping

Whenever possible, try to camp in areas that have been used as campsites before. This is safer and more practical. Setting up a campsite in a new location can be a lot of work and it's hard to do without leaving some scars on the landscape. Regardless of how adept someone becomes at no-trace camping, it doesn't mean that it's okay to camp whereever they wish because they believe they won't leave any traces. It's virtually impossible to spend a night at a campsite without leaving some indication that someone camped there. Setting up camp in an area that's never been used before is something that should only be done in emergency situations or in deep wilderness where there are no established campsites. The motto for wilderness travelers should be "take only photographs, leave only footprints."

With proper risk management, taking children into the wilderness by canoe is safer than taking them to the movies by automobile. Good pre-trip preparation ensures their safety.

Chapter 8

· · · · · · · · · · · · · · · · · ·

Playing It Safe

*I*T SEEMS TO BE A COMMONLY HELD BELIEF THAT WILDERNESS-tripping is a risky business in which you leave the comforts of civilization and go out to battle the elements. The boring truth of the matter is that with proper preparation, wilderness travel is no more dangerous than a trip to the shopping mall.

To reduce risks, you need to have a plan in place in case something should go wrong and have the knowledge and skills to implement this plan. Proper preparation for outdoor adventures means being able to travel in safety and comfort under almost any circumstances, no matter what the weather does, no matter what surprises are encountered. The most important key to returning home in one piece with your pride intact is to fix little problems before they become big ones.

Crisis Prevention

It is impossible to eliminate all risks from our lives, so we must learn to manage them. Crisis management is knowing what to do when something has gone tragically wrong. This means not only being prepared with the skills and tools to take care of medical emergencies or search and rescue, but also making sure that there are back-up plans in place in case something happens to the person who would normally be responsible for taking care of emergencies. In a family situation, both parents should be familiar enough with emergency procedures that either could take over. Accidents and sudden illnesses can happen anytime, and its best to have a plan organized and procedures rehearsed.

Risk management

Risk management is the process of taking care of little problems before they become big ones. Good risk management involves maintaining a heightened awareness of your surroundings and the things that are happening around you. Wilderness tragedies are rarely the result of one major catastrophe. Major incidents are usually the result of a chain of lesser events. The small incidents are mistakes in judgment or minor occurrences that would be easy to deal with on their own. If the chain of events is broken early, there are seldom any problems that can't be dealt with. Left to continue, the sequence continues to build until eventually it leads to tragedy.

Pre-planning

Pre-planning relies on the camper's past experience and personal research to anticipate any problems that might happen on a trip. As you spend more time outdoors, you will gradually develop a library of solutions to a variety of problems. From the experience gained over time, it becomes easier to anticipate problems that you haven't encountered before. Pre-planning also involves determining what you will need for any outdoor adventure. If pre-planning and risk management are properly taken care of, odds are that crisis management will never be required.

Before heading out

Pre-trip planning means playing devil's advocate, imagining how a minor inconvenience can escalate into a real problem. A simple thing like a loose screw that could have been tightened in a matter of minutes can turn into a broken piece of equipment that creates a problem that might cause the loss of equipment or even the loss of a life.

Before heading out on a canoe trip with your children, it is important to think about what could go wrong and to identify possible solutions. While it may not be a comfortable feeling, facing the thought of such things and creating hypothetical life-threatening situations, it is much better to find workable solutions in an abstract setting such as your living room than it is to solve a crisis while it's happening.

Creating and using checklists is a good start to your pre-planning. When you are making these checklists or modifying them, you are forced to begin to think about some of the things that you will encounter on the canoe trip with your child.

Making lists

When you start out traveling in the wilderness, you'll find that you brought some things that weren't necessary and forgot some things that you should have brought. There is a certain amount of experimentation involved in finding the right balance between having enough stuff to meet your needs, yet keeping your packs small enough to fit into a canoe or light enough to be carried over the portage. Keeping a list of the things that you have packed and making notes about items that could be left behind or items that were missed helps to improve future trips. The longer and more remote the trip, the greater the importance of the list.

There would be nothing wrong with using one long list for all the things required on a trip, but we find it more practical to create smaller lists that are more task-oriented, i.e. a food list, an equipment list, a clothing list, a first-aid list, etc. That way it's easier to adjust for changing factors such as destinations, seasons or mode of travel. We keep a copy of the first-aid list packed in the kit and we keep several copies of the food and menus in the food packs. A master list can contain all the items that you might need for the full range of seasons and destinations. With this sort of list, items that won't be needed can be stroked off before you start gathering equipment.

It's unlikely that you'll find a checklist in a publication (even this one!) that suites your needs perfectly. Published lists are only guide-lines. Modify them and creating your own checklists to meet the needs of your family.

First-aid

What goes into a first-aid kit depends on where you're going. For short trips in semi-wilderness, a comprehensive first-aid kit may not be as critical. Hospitals and emergency transportation aren't that far away, and in all likelihood, there's a good chance help will be nearby.

In a medical emergency, the goal is to stabilize the injury and transport the casualty to qualified medical help as soon as possible. In most accident situations involving the family, there usually isn't enough time to grab the first-aid kit, a solution usually needs to be improvised from materials readily at hand. After the situation is stable, there's time to get the first-aid kit out of the pack and dispense whatever bandages or medication are required.

On canoe trips, the first-aid kit is actually more of a second-aid kit. Instead of trying to prepare for every emergency, kits for semi-wilderness travel should concentrate on remedies that will keep trippers comfortable. The kit should include things such as bandages, allergy medication, painkillers, elastic wraps and something to look after mild infections and to clean wounds.

The first-aid kit should be kept in an accessible location at all times. This is especially true when traveling with children. The middle of the night seems to be one of the most common times when they need attention. Keep at least a minimal kit with some bandages and painkillers in a childproof container in the tent overnight.

On most trips, we usually take supplies to deal with pain, to cover wounds, reduce swelling, wrap muscles, protect or soothe irritated skin, and to remove slivers. Be sure to include the following:

- Acetaminophen (Tylenol) for pain and fevers (both adult and child formulas).
- ASA (Aspirin) for pain and to reduce the swelling in joints and tendons (tennis elbow is a common ailment among canoeists). ASA may be helpful to the adults, but shouldn't be given to children or teens.
- Zinc oxide for skin irritations and skin protection. If you have an infant, make sure that the first-aid kit includes something to take care of diaper rash. Some zinc oxide is a useful remedy for this problem. It can also be used for a variety of other first-aid needs and act as a sunblock to prevent sunburn.
- Tweezers for slivers. Children are prone to slivers, and having the right tools on hand to remove them quickly is important. Carry a small pair of scissors and a good pair of tweezers in the first-aid kit.
- Bandages for a variety of ailments, such as blisters, sprained ankles, wounds, and gauze wraps for wounds or burns. Duct tape and toilet paper make a great Band-Aid in a pinch, but it's harder to get off later.

- Antiseptic soaps for cleansing wounds. Secondary infections often cause more problems than the initial injury. Cleaning a wound thoroughly and keeping it clean is important.
- Petroleum jelly is useful for cracked or dry skin as well as for keeping bandages from sticking to burns.
- Antihistamines are always included in our kit to help reduce the swelling resulting from a mild allergic reaction, especially to insect bites. While cold compresses will help to relieve swelling, it is handy to have some medication that can also assist with this. Various people react differently to antihistamines. Be sure you know of any adverse reactions before you administer them to your child in the wilderness.

Dealing with insects

Insect bites are a common problem on wilderness trips. Allergic reactions can cause swelling, sometimes severe enough to interfere with breathing. An antihistamine can help reduce the swelling associated with most bites. In some cases, the first few blackfly or mosquito bites of the season can cause enough swelling that eyes are reduced to mere slits. As the camping season progresses, kids usually develop a tolerance for bug bites, but until they do, parents should monitor them carefully.

It is important to keep in mind that the first bite from an insect usually isn't the one that causes severe allergic reactions. Just because a youngster has been stung or bitten by an insect once and didn't appear to be adversely affected, it is no grounds to relax your concerns. The second bee sting is the most dangerous one.

Be cautious about using insect repellents on children, and never apply repellents on infants under six months of age. The active ingredient in many insect repellents is DEET, and it is possible to purchase repellents that contain percentages of that active ingredient approaching 100 percent. Don't use high concentrations on children. Look for ones that contain between ten and forty percent DEET. Parents need to be cautious about applying repellent, as young children can get DEET into their mouths or eyes by rubbing their hands over areas where the repellent was used. A mild repellent in a pump dispenser can be used to lightly spray clothing instead of skin. Some parents may elect to use "natural" products such as Citronella. This may be an option for some, but a person who is sensitive to plants and perfumes may not be able to use these products.

If you do not want to use repellents, it's best to prevent bites by keeping the children covered. Long sleeves and pant legs are a big help in keeping bugs off. Keep pants tucked into socks to prevent insects from biting the lower legs. Light-colored clothing seems to attract fewer insects than dark clothing, and it's easier to see bugs such as ticks on the light clothing. Using a bandanna around the neck or tucked under a baseball cap can prevent a lot of insect bites around the neck and ears. Some new outdoor clothing is made from tightly woven fabrics that bugs cannot bite through. Some garments have been designed specifically to keep bugs at bay. But make sure they are wearing it properly all the time. As they play, the clothing can ride up and expose areas of tender flesh that biting insects find tempting.

There are various kinds of insects that bite and some bites are of more concern than others. On a recent trip above the Arctic Circle, we were forced to lay over for a day while we waited to see if a spider bite was going become an emergency. Spiders weren't a hazard that we were expecting above the Arctic Circle, but one was hiding under a small stuff sack where the gear was laid out in the sand. The spider bit the hand that picked up the stuff sack as the gear was being gathered that morning. The pain from the bite was excruciating and the hand became quite swollen. Keeping the swollen hand lowered in cool arctic water helped. Fortunately, it didn't get any worse and we were able to continue. Medical help was a long way away and there really wasn't a lot we could have done. In this case, it was an unavoidable risk.

People who have severe allergic reactions should carry a sting kit (Epi-pen) with them and make sure that other members of the canoeing party know where it's kept and what to do with it if the owner becomes incapacitated.

Kids will often want to bring their friends along with them on camping trips. It is imperative that you find out from the child's parents if there are any medical problems that you should be aware of before you take them with you.

Burns
Accidental burns can be one of the most serious problems to deal with. There is no substitute for good training to learn how to deal with

Taking children into the wilderness means it's important to minimize risks. That doesn't mean avoiding interesting natural phenomenon such as these gypsum caves on the lower Missinabi River, just be extra cautious.

burns. Children are naturally fascinated with fires, and parents must pay extra attention any time a fire is burning or food is being heated.

Most camp stoves are fairly small to make them easy to pack. While the small size is a great advantage to the camper, it often means that large pots are relatively unstable when they're being heated on the stove. Having a large pot full of hot liquid balanced precariously on a small stove creates a dangerous situation. This can be made much safer by building a structure of rocks around the stove or using a grill to support the weight and steady the pot.

If a burn does happen, the first thing to do is to cool the burn area as much as possible. On a canoe trip, the easiest way to do this is to take the victim down to the water and immerse the entire area of the burn. Try to keep the area of the burn immersed until the burning sensation stops. More severe burns victims can lead to a state of great distress or panic, so the victim may have to be calmed down and reassured. Don't react to their panic. Cool off the burned area as quickly as possible to reduce the extent of the damage. Provide painkillers as necessary for the pain.

Once the immediate care of the burn has been attended to, the next concern is preventing any infection. Depending on the location and the extent of the burn, medical attention may be warranted. If the nature of the trip prevents prompt medical attention, bandage the burn with sterile dressings. As long as the skin covering the burn stays intact, the chance of an infection is minimal.

Burns result in blisters. The skin covering a blister is fragile, so it's important that nothing sticks to it or brushes against, because it must remain intact to act as a barrier against infection. This presents a challenge in bandaging. Some good commercial bandages are specifically designed to deal with burns. A good first-aid kit should contain some of these bandages. If the burn area is too large or the length of the trip is such that the supply of bandages doesn't allow for proper bandaging of the burn, you'll have to resort to some ingenuity. Petroleum jelly slathered onto the gauze bandage will lessen the likelihood of bandages sticking to the skin. Constructing a donut of bandage material or other cloth and taping it in place around the burn area will help prevent direct pressure on the skin and give some support to the blister.

Hot and cold

Young children are generally more affected by changes in air temperature than adults are.

Hypothermia is when a person's internal temperature drops too far for the body to function properly. When a person is in a frigid environment, their body starts to conserve heat by shutting down circulation of blood to the skin and extremities so that heat can be maintained in the core organs and that oxygen-rich blood will continue to be pumped to the brain. If the body continues to drop in temperature, eventually it will affect the function of the brain and organs. Hypothermia can happen easily in the winter, but it can also happen on what would seem to be a warm summer day. Parents need to watchful for the early signs of hypothermia in their children.

The first indication of hypothermia is a change in color of the lips or fingertips. Shivering is the next phase. If a child begins to shiver, they should be warmed up immediately. Keep them sheltered from the wind; bundle them up in warm clothing, especially in the areas that concentrate heat — the head, the armpits, the groin and the torso. During this initial phase, one of the best ways to generate some heat is to feed them something warm to eat or drink. Warm food and drink provide direct heat, as well as secondary heat generated through digestion. Once the person has regained their body heat, they'll be fine, but they will be more prone to losing the heat they have just regained, so they should be watched carefully until their temperature is well stabilized. Dealing with the early stages is easy and prompt attention will prevent serious problems.

Hyperthermia is when the body's internal temperature gets too warm. For canoeists and outdoor enthusiasts the most common reason for a person to overheat is because their clothing has interfered with the body's natural evaporation of sweat. Overexertion, especially on hot and humid days, can make the problem worse.

With hyperthermia, a flushed red face and excessive sweating are two signs to watch for. Unusually dry diapers or changes to a normal schedule of washroom breaks are another good indication of the early stages of hyperthermia. Dehydration happens because the body is losing a lot of fluid through sweat. Strong smelling or richly colored urine also indicate that a person is becoming dehydrated. Dehydration and hyperthermia usually go hand in hand.

If a person exhibits these clues, it is important to cool them immediately and help them to rehydrate. Children need to be watched carefully. Because they are usually bundled up in their lifejackets and they do not seem to sweat as profusely as adults do, the early warning signs may be overlooked. Once the sweating seems to stop, the person has slipped into a more dangerous phase and should be given immediate medical attention. Fortunately on a canoe trip, the early stages of hyperthermia are easy to take care of — just take a swimming break. Simply wearing a hat or bandanna that has been soaked in water can also keep hyperthermia from setting in. Find some shade and get the person to relax.

Bumps and scrapes

Parents are never going to be in a position to prevent the bumps and scrapes that happen to their children. That's an unavoidable part of growing up. We can, however, lessen the risk of injury several ways. One of the things we discovered early on was that our kids had extra

Wilderness rivers, such as the White River flowing into Lake Superior, cut through rough terrain, which creates an obstacle course for pint-sized paddlers. Keeping a PFD on children helps lessen cuts and bruises if they trip.

padding if we left their lifejackets on them. The lifejackets helped a lot in protecting them from bumps and scrapes when they fell.

It's a good idea to fasten little bells to children when they're starting to become more mobile. The bell helps to keep track of what's happening if your attention is momentarily taken up by something else.

Treating bumps and scrapes in the wilderness isn't really any different than at home. Check out any bumps for any signs of problems and pay close attention to any bumps on the head. For scrapes, just clean thoroughly with soap and water, then bandage to keep the dirt out.

Getting lost

Getting lost can happen to anybody, regardless of their experience or skill. Parents on a canoe trip have to make sure that their children are safe, but they have the added responsibility of making sure that they don't put themselves in a position where they might get lost themselves. That means that extra care must be taken even for mundane tasks such as collecting firewood or finding a good place to use as a toilet.

Search efforts for lost people rely on the use of grid patterns to ensure the lost person isn't missed. If a child is wandering, they may be missed when the search grid is checked, so it's important that you find ways to make them stay put. Tell them to find a tree they like and make friends with it. It will provide them with some comfort and keep them in one spot until they are found. Each child should be outfitted with a whistle. They should be trained to use the whistle to signal problems and not use it as a toy. Three blasts of the whistle is the standard signal for distress, and the child should be trained to use this signal.

Make sure that the child knows that no matter how long it takes, someone will come to find them. The child needs to know that if they get lost, they must stay where they are and they should try to guide searchers to them by blowing their whistle or making noises if they hear or see anyone. Unfortunately, the streetproofing that children get at home and in school often conflicts with what they need to do if they're lost. It may well be a stranger who first discovers the lost child, and children have been known to hide from searchers they did not know. Take time to explain the difference.

Some people have a better sense of direction than others do. Test your child's ability to visualize their whereabouts by asking where non-visible landmarks are. This can be as simple as asking which way home is when you're driving to the shopping mall. During camping trips, use opportunities such as portages to check your child's sense of direction. If the child is good at visualizing their location, it means they are less likely to get turned around when you're out in the wild.

Emergency communication

For some people, one of the goals in wilderness travel is to escape from civilization. While there are a lot of good reasons for wanting to do this, it is a good idea to have a communication link back to civilization in case something goes wrong. Some people are reluctant to bring a communication device along because they believe that this will lessen their sense of isolation, which is an important part of traveling in the wild for them. If one of your camping goals is to teach your children about independence and self-reliance, you may want to keep the radio or cell phone hidden until the kids are older. Having a communication device along but never taking it out of the pack could be a compromise.

Keep in mind that rivers usually flow through valleys and that this can lower the signal strength of cell phones. Do some research on what sort of coverage you might expect in the area you will be traveling through. Cell phones will not work in remote wilderness, as there are no relay towers in these areas. Check the signal strength occasionally along your route.

For remote wilderness travel, emergency communication equipment usually takes the form of either a one-way signaling device, such as the Emergency Locating Transmitter (ELT) used to locate aircraft that have crashed, or two-way communication devices such as satellite phones or radios.

For canoe parties traveling into remote areas, the most commonly used signaling device is an Emergency Position Indicating Radio Beacon (EPIRB). These send out a signal that is directed to the Search and Rescue Satellite-Aided Tracking (SARSAT) crews for response. Because more people are going out into the wilderness and false alarms are a significant drain on emergency response systems, parties that send out a false alarm stand a good chance of being billed for the service. The cost of some rescue operations would be enough to pay for a good-sized house in many communities. Wilderness travelers need to take every possible precaution to avoid being the cause of an unnecessary search. Make sure that the device is secured in such a way that it couldn't possibly go off accidentally.

Though they're expensive, by far the most reliable option for communication in the wilderness are satellite phones. These phones will work just about anywhere, and the quality of audio is not much different than the cordless phone in your home.

On a recent canoe trip on a remote river above the Arctic Circle, we brought along a satellite phone. There is no denying that having the phone with us changed our sense of isolation. Within moments, we could dial up and speak to anybody we wished. Our goal was to only use it in an emergency and to assure the folks back home that we were safe. Sunday phone calls were a welcome reassurance for our families at home. We used the phone to call the float plane base to make sure the aircraft was coming to pick us up after a month on the river. There were several times on the trip when we joked about phoning one of the pizza companies that promise free delivery if they're late.

Regardless of the type of communication device that you choose to accompany you and your family on a canoe trip, keeping it stored in something that will keep it dry. Delicate phone or radio components that get wet may never work again.

Parents often worry about bringing enough toys for kids. No need to worry, they have great imaginations and will find hours of play in found objects like these caribou antlers on the Horton River, NWT.

Chapter 9
·····················
Camp Games & Entertainment

SO NOW THAT WE HAVE THE KIDS OUT HERE WITH US, WHAT DO we do with them? Many parents are concerned about entertaining their children while they are in the canoe or at the campsite. Uncertainty over what to do on rainy days can be a deterrent to even venturing out with children. Left to their own devices, children are quite capable of amusing themselves, but it's not a bad idea to have some tricks up your sleeve.

Baby, that's entertainment
For the most part, babies are content when they can look around and see their parents nearby. When carrying them on a portage, tie one of their teething rings by a short string to the front of the backpack carrier. This way they have something to chew on besides your hair.

Wearing a hat that is covered with bright, colorful animals or faces may not necessarily be your choice in fashion, but it is likely to be a hit with young infants. As their vision is limited, they tend to focus on bright colors, shapes and faces. If you can't buy an entertaining hat, you can redecorate a plain one with fabric paints and textured patches such as fun fur or terry cloth.

Rattle socks are a great invention. You can make your own version of these by sewing small, inexpensive rattles into a sleeve of fabric attached to regular infant socks These are a must for on a canoe trip with small infants. They can also be worn as mittens.

As the child gets a little older, a stroller activity toy with lots of colorful balls and rattles can be stretched across the canoe.

Babies love songs. Generally it doesn't matter whether or not you remember the right words. It is the melody and the rhythm that infants respond to. Listening to tapes of children's songs can help you remember the words. There's also nothing wrong with singing your favorite pop or folk songs to infants as you paddle along.

On sunny afternoons, let your baby splash in the water. Protect their delicate skin from the sun by dressing them in a long-sleeve T-shirt and a wide-brimmed hat. If the water's edge looks too dangerous, you can still have water play by using a wash basin on a tarp. Using the wash-basin method, the water can be warmed by the sun for a half-hour before baby gets in it. For older children, a sturdy canoe can serve as a bathtub.

One of the main reasons for going out camping with infants is to stimulate their senses and to experience some quality family time. With this in mind, set up camp early and spend time lying in the hammock hugging your baby. This bonding time will lead both of you to enjoy the wilderness and the peace of nature.

Toddler fun starts at home

The fun of canoeing for toddlers starts at home. Paddling their beds and portaging laundry baskets around the house was a favorite pastime for our boys.

Toddlers love to empty things and fill them up again. Bringing along a small pail and shovel can entertain youngsters for hours.

While portaging, sing silly fun songs to help the toddler keep going. Songs that you can keep a walking pace to are great. A used margarine tub with a few pine cones or stones creates a rattle or tambourine for accompaniment. The hard part for many adults is just thinking up the songs. Keep a recipe card with song titles in your pocket to jog your memory.

Toddlers like to mimic the "big people." So if a big sister or an adult is fishing, they will probably want to get in on the action. A wooden fish tied to the end of a small piece of string on the end of a wooden pole is as close to the real thing as many toddlers require.

Kids can't seem to avoid playing in mud at the end of a portage while the adults are shuttling gear. Mud patties are fun to make, but the end of the portage is the place where many animals also enter and exit the water. This could be a problem because animal droppings may cause high bacterial counts. In addition, leeches are often found in these areas. If a child does encounter a leech, simply remove it by sprinkling it generously with salt. This will cause the leach to let go and drop off.

Making sandcastles is a safer activity. Sandy beaches are cleaner for toddlers to play in. If you happen upon a sandy beach as you are paddling, stop for a while. These breaks allow the toddler time to get out of the canoe and give them a chance to run off some energy. You will both benefit.

Toddlers naturally start tossing stones in the water. The goal for toddlers is simply to let go of the stone at the right time. Throwing is something that adults take for granted, but this is a milestone in a child's physical development. They can spend hours of practicing and refining this skill.

Besides obvious building opportunities, stone beaches offer treasure-hunting toddlers countless other opportunities. Putting little rocks into a bucket and dumping them out again is a lot of fun for toddlers. Encourage them to be selective, collecting only pink rocks or only egg-shaped rocks, to extend the child's sorting and classifying skills. Some of these nice, clean rocks can be brought inside a tent for rainy afternoon play. Make sure the stones won't create a choking hazard.

Stick boats are another toddler favorite. Any stick will do, but the opportunity to collect a few little twigs along the portage for stick boats may encourage a toddler to walk along on their own instead of wanting to be carried.

Toddlers are superb observers. Perhaps it is because they are so low to the ground, but they seem to be keenly aware of the wonders of the insect world at our feet. The "look don't touch" philosophy helps residents of the insect world a lot. Teach your child to simply observe insects in their natural environment. They will learn more and it will prevent injury to the insects.

Nature rubbings are easy to do and the artwork is instant. Put some plain paper on something with a lot of texture, such as a rock, a tree trunk or a leaf placed on a hard surface. Using the side of a crayon, scribble or rub all over the paper. The impression of the object behind the paper starts to come through almost like magic. The biggest problem with nature rubbings is the amount of paper that you will need because the child's nature rubbings are likely to be prolific.

Include a pack or two of cards. Card games such as "Go Fish" and "Old Maid" can be used for memory matching games for youngsters.

Preoccupying the preschooler

Preschoolers have difficulty following rules, but they are creatures of habit and routine. Develop some family traditions. These can range from the singing of favorite songs as soon as everyone is in their tents for the night, to a special or funny poem recited when a portage is completed. Such traditions are personal, so have fun and be creative.

Preschoolers' sandcastles and rock castles may include stick bridges and moats filled with water. Parents may need to offer a few renovation suggestions on occasion, or they may prefer to get into the action and help out with the building. This is another great learning opportunity and a good way to spend time together.

Older preschool children are physically able to begin learning the fine art of rock skipping. This skill can be practiced for many years to come, with no upper age limit. Looking for the perfect round and flat skipping rock can take place on a portage as well as at camp. This is an opportunity for adults to play at throwing rocks under the guise of teaching their preschooler. Just one word of advice, though, older shoulders may need a bit of a warm up before letting that impressive double-digit sidewinding skipper go.

Simple but fun games such as Thumb Wars, I Spy, and Paper, Rock, Scissors can be great diversions. The Naming Game is an activity that can last for hours, and it is often amazing to listen to your child list off things that the adults have never heard of. The object of the Naming Game is to list off as many things that fit under a particular category as you can remember. For example, "Name as many kinds of candies as you can." After the first player has completed the list, they get to choose the topic for the next person.

We let our children select one toy each to take on a trip, but we often also packed a brightly colored Nerf ball or a Koosh ball. These balls weigh hardly anything, compress to nothing, and don't bounce or roll far when they are dropped.

For bedtime, we encouraged the kids to bring a hand puppet rather than a small stuffed toy. There is more play value in a puppet, and the adults and children both can have fun telling stories with the puppet, yet it can still be a soft bedtime toy. If it just doesn't feel the same to the child, stuff a clean pair of socks into the puppet for night-time cuddling.

School-age spirit

School-age children can share in storytelling activities during long car rides, or while paddling across lakes, or sitting around the campfire. A nice twist is to use an improvisation technique used by some comedians. One person starts telling a story and stops midway through a sentence. The next person has to finish the interrupted sentence and continue the story for a few more sentences before stopping midsentence and handing it on to the next person.

A variation is the Alphabet Conversation. A continuing story is told with each person delivering one sentence each time they get a turn. Starting anywhere in the alphabet, the first person begins the conversation with a letter of the alphabet. The next person must take over and continue the conversation with a sentence that must start with the next letter in the alphabet. For example, starting at the letter "H," the first person says, "Hello, fancy meeting you here." The next person says, "I'm happy to see you again," which starts with the letter "I." Followed by the next person saying, "Jump in, we are going for a canoe ride." And so on.

Balsam boat races were popular with our boys. The kids must first find some sticks that they think will make good boats, then scout around for a balsam fir tree that has sap seeping out of openings in its bark. They should scoop a little of the sticky sap on the end of a stick and return to the water. When their boat is placed on a calm stretch of water, it's just a matter seconds before the stick boat will start to move as balsam gum's oily chemicals spread out on the water.

When the child is old enough to safely handle a knife, carving and whittling their own boat or canoe can be a lot of fun. When our boys were eight and eleven we took along a Swiss Army knife for each of them when we went on month-long canoe trip. We selected knives that had locking blades, so there was no chance of an accident if they applied pressure on the wrong side of the blade. After lots of instruction on how to handle knives safely, we all got some pieces of softwood carved miniature canoes. Collecting firewood became an occasion to also look for a perfect piece of fallen cedar, basswood or spruce that they could bring back to the campsite to carve. The boys spent hours playing with their new handcrafted toy canoes.

Yo-yos are a fun toy that don't take up much room. Hopscotch requires no materials except a couple of different colored stones and a hopscotch board scratched into the sand on the beach. A few marbles in a pouch will take up little space and can challenge the flicking skills between younger and older generations. A few props and a book on magic tricks can also be a fun way to pass idle time.

Skipping is another activity that requires little equipment. Chances are, there's a short rope somewhere in your camp kit that can be used for skipping. To prevent twisted ankles, make sure skipping takes place on a level surface.

Reading and writing are activities that need to be encouraged at any time, and canoeing excursions can offer an opportune time to write and read with purpose. Keeping a daily journal to describe the day's events is a good activity for parent and child to share in the tent. The journal can be done in words but can also include sketches. Writing captions at the bottom of the drawings will help to preserve the memories of key events on the trip. Some children may prefer to create a running cartoon with dialogue boxes briefly explaining the days events.

Some children will delight in bringing along a book to read in their tent on a rainy day. For others, whose favorite pastime is not reading, bringing along a few plant or animal identification books will encourage reading skills while fostering their natural curiosity.

As a child's memory improves, longer campfire songs can become part of their repertoire. It is amazing how far you can paddle without even realizing it when you are singing a long story-oriented song. The nice thing about being out in the wilderness is that moose really don't care if you can carry a tune.

As long as a game does not require cards of clues or directions, you can often make your own homemade board. With the exception of a pair of dice, which you will need to bring from home, nature provides all sorts of game pieces - colored stones, pieces of sticks, acorns, maple keys, etc.

Knot-tying is a skill that can be shared with your school-age child.

As they learn to tie their shoes, they also develop the concepts necessary to learn about various types of knots. Choose some easy knots, such as the half hitch, the square knot or the bowline, and share them with your child.

Fishing is a great pastime. Our boys love to troll from a canoe (mostly because this means they don't have to paddle). We like to indulge them as long as time is not an issue. They seem to enjoy the process of fishing whether or not they catch anything. Our "fishing rules" included wearing a lifejacket at all times, removing lures or hooks from fishing rods when they were not in use, keeping the rods in a safe place, and asking permission to go fishing in a specific location that they won't wander from. This way we could determine if their fishing site posed any hazards.

One canoeing related skill that is important to develop is mapreading. Sit down at the end of the portage and look at the map together to determine where you need to go next. This not only helps to develop mapreading skills but can also develop mutual respect.

Older children may enjoy exploring their creative side through the lens of a camera. A pre-teen is ready to begin learning the basics of photography. As the child takes pictures, they are creating their own personal record of their trip. This is something they can put into a photo album, write captions about, and show their friends from school. Another interest that may be fostered through photography is plant or animal identification.

Bringing your child's friend or a cousin along may make camping a more rewarding experience and gives the child an opportunity to show off their skills. Unlike involvement in group sports such as hockey or baseball, canoeing is something that is often hidden from peers. This gives your child the opportunity to feel proud of all the camping skills they have learned.

Older teens may no longer want to go canoeing with their parents. Rather, they'll borrow the canoe, the car and the tent, and head off with their friends. Although it may not help you sleep at night as you toss and turn, worried about them, at least you will know that you have instilled in them a sense of respect and pleasure in being out in the wilderness. Knowing that they have absorbed years of camp skills may help you to know that the canoe, the tent, and everyone will return safely.

*Taking children into the wilderness isn't without challenge or risk.
Many might wonder if it's worth it. To us, there probably isn't a better
way to form a close and lasting friendship with your kids.*

Conclusion

*T*HE RED CANOE GLIDED SILENTLY IN THE FLOODED FOREST OF the swamp, bathed in the warm sunlight, surrounded by the choir of birds greeting the dawn of a new season. It was mid-March and the sleepy-eyed muskrats drifted on floating platforms of reeds, savoring the bounty of tender new growth springing to life in their watery domain below. As the bleak days of winter transformed magically to the blossoming days of spring, our lives also experienced a change. Bundled in warm clothes to shed the brisk chill in the morning air, our infant son rested contently in the cradle of the canoe. In years gone by, we had come to the wilderness as paddlers, on this day we came as parents.

And so began the first day of a new life for us.

Traveling in the wilderness with children isn't always easy. Leaving the safety and comfort of home in exchange for the uncertainty of a campsite can be unsettling for a parent, no matter how well prepared they are.

Key among the reasons why people want to venture into the wilderness with their children is the opportunity to relax and enjoy each other's company, something that becomes increasingly difficult in day-to-day living. But don't expect to be able to head out on a two-week canoe trip with children who have never been in a canoe. Start gradually and let everyone get accustomed to the idea of being in a canoe in the outdoors. Short but happy excursions will help the family to acquire the confidence so that they will be able to make more extensive journeys.

The investment of time and effort in taking children outdoors brings many rewards. These rewards may not always be tangible, but they are priceless. Building memories together helps to bond parents and their children. In contrast to the hustle of everyday life, going camping helps everyone slow down and open their eyes to each other and to the wonders of nature. Adjusting our rhythms to the natural

world has a soothing, calming effect that makes it easier to relate to other people.

One of the things that we didn't expect was that our boys would become such good friends. They each enjoyed helping their brother improve his skills or learn more about nature. As they grew older, their observations became more insightful, and we enjoyed sharing their fresh perspectives on a world we thought we knew well. It has been interesting for us to watch their development and learn what has been most important to them.

Brendan tells us that he especially enjoys the time with his family. He adds, "Paddling helps me get stronger. It takes time to learn how to paddle properly, so don't think that it will be easy, but keep trying because it is fun when you actually get it right."

Kyle enjoys the travel: "I like to go and see different parts of the world with the canoeing I do." And his is perhaps the best testimonial for this book: "When I grow up, I want to take my kids canoeing because I know they will like camping."

It's a bit frightening the first time you take your children into the wilderness. But with the proper preparation and a bit of co-operation from the weather, it will be the first step in a journey that will last a lifetime. The experiences a family can have in the outdoors has a profound effect on the bond that holds them together. Our children summarize this well: "Home is wherever the whole family is together."

Checklists

These lists are useful for all camping trips whether you are car camping or canoe camping. Each list is only a general guideline. You will want to modify these for your own camping trips.

- MASTER CAMPING CHECKLISTS

- DAY TRIP CHECKLIST

- KITCHEN CHECKLIST

- CLOTHING CHECKLIST

- FIRST-AID / MEDICAL SUPPLIES

- BABY NEEDS

- REPAIR KIT

- COAST GUARD REQUIREMENTS

- SEVEN-DAY MENU PLANNER

These checklists may be duplicated by the original purchasers for personal use only.

Master Camping Checklists

KITCHEN

- ❏ stove
- ❏ fuel
- ❏ funnel for fuel
- ❏ cups   (#_____)
- ❏ plates   (#_____)
- ❏ bowls   (#_____)
- ❏ knives   (#_____)
- ❏ forks   (#_____)
- ❏ spoons   (#_____)
- ❏ sharp knife
- ❏ cutting board
- ❏ can opener
- ❏ vegetable peeler
- ❏ large spoon
- ❏ lifter
- ❏ whisk
- ❏ pots   (#_____)
- ❏ fry pan
- ❏ pot lifter
- ❏ fire bar/grate
- ❏ matches
- ❏ lighter

- ❏ fire starter
- ❏ water filter
- ❏ replacement filter
- ❏ water bottle   (#_____)
- ❏ dish pan
- ❏ powder bleach
- ❏ dish soap
- ❏ dish towels   (#_____)
- ❏ dish cloth   (#_____)
- ❏ scratch pad
- ❏ leather work gloves
- ❏ cup-size coffee filter
- ❏ reflector oven
- ❏ outback oven

- ❏ _____
- ❏ _____
- ❏ _____
- ❏ _____

SLEEPING

- ❏ tent (#_____ & size_____)
- ❏ sleeping bag   (#_____)
- ❏ sleeping pad   (#_____)
- ❏ candle lantern
- ❏ "pee pot"
- ❏ pillow?   (#_____)
- ❏ flashlights

- ❏ _____
- ❏ _____
- ❏ _____
- ❏ _____

PACKS

- ❑ Packs (#_____)
- ❑ waterproof pack (#_____)
- ❑ stuff sacks (#_____)
- ❑ compression stuff sacks
- ❑ _____
- ❑ _____

ADDITIONAL

- ❑ health cards / insurance
- ❑ first aid kit
- ❑ zinc oxide
- ❑ sun screen (15+)
- ❑ bug repellent
- ❑ bug jacket (#_____)
- ❑ umbrella
- ❑ hammock
- ❑ axe/saw
- ❑ carabiners
- ❑ ropes various lengths
- ❑ toilet paper (# rolls_____)
- ❑ small lantern
- ❑ tarps (#_____ & size_____)
- ❑ camera equipment
- ❑ camera film
- ❑ communication device (cellphone, 2-way radio, etc)
- ❑ blank journal, book and pen
- ❑ _____
- ❑ _____
- ❑ _____

CLOTHING PER PERSON

- ❑ underwear (#_____)
- ❑ t-shirts (#_____)
- ❑ shorts (#_____)
- ❑ long pants (#_____)
- ❑ socks (#_____)
- ❑ long-sleeve shirt (#_____)
- ❑ warm upper (#_____)
- ❑ warm lower (#_____)
- ❑ rain gear
- ❑ bandanas
- ❑ sun hat
- ❑ sunglasses
- ❑ bathing suit
- ❑ towel
- ❑ warm jacket
- ❑ gloves
- ❑ mitts
- ❑ fleece hat
- ❑ fleece socks
- ❑ wet shoes
- ❑ dry shoes
- ❑ GoreTex sock (optional)
- ❑ _____
- ❑ _____
- ❑ _____

PERSONAL ITEMS

- ❏ toothbrush
- ❏ toothpaste
- ❏ hair brush
- ❏ medication
- ❏ glasses
- ❏ contact – solutions/case

- ❏ _____
- ❏ _____
- ❏ _____

CANOEING

- ❏ canoe   (#_____)
- ❏ PFD   (#_____)
- ❏ paddles –
  type _____ (#_____)
- ❏ bailer
- ❏ whistle (one per person)
- ❏ maps
- ❏ compass
- ❏ buoyant heaving device –
  50 feet (floating rope)
- ❏ route plan

- ❏ emergency aid locations
- ❏ safety contact who has
  itinerary and route plan:
  _____
- ❏ phone #:
  _____
- ❏ _____
- ❏ _____

FOOD PACK

- ❏ juice crystals
- ❏ menu
- ❏ salt, pepper, _____spices
- ❏ lunches   (#_____)
- ❏ breakfasts   (#_____)
- ❏ dinners   (#_____)
- ❏ snacks
- ❏ GORP

- ❏ hard candy
- ❏ infant formula
- ❏ infant foods
- ❏ beverages
- ❏ _____
- ❏ _____

Day Trip Checklist

❏ canoe (#_____)
❏ PFD (#_____)
❏ paddles-
  type _____ (#_____)
❏ bailer
❏ whistle
❏ maps
❏ compass
❏ buoyant heaving device –
  50 feet (floating rope)
❏ route plan
❏ emergency aid locations
❏ safety contact who has
  itinerary and route plan:

  _____

❏ phone #:

  _____

❏ first-aid kit
❏ personal medications
❏ sunscreen (15+)
❏ sunglasses
❏ hats
❏ umbrella for shade
❏ rain gear
❏ bug jackets
❏ insect repellent
❏ snack / lunch

❏ water filter
❏ water bottles
❏ juice crystals
❏ juice boxes
❏ toilet paper
❏ health cards / insurance
❏ matches / lighter
❏ repair kit
❏ small tarp
❏ rope
❏ toilet seat for toddlers
❏ diapers
❏ infant bottles and powder
  formula
❏ mosquito netting for feeding
  baby
❏ communication device (cell
  phone)

❏ _____

❏ _____

❏ _____

❏ _____

Kitchen Checklist

- ❑ stove
- ❑ fuel for _____ days
  - quantity needed _____
- ❑ funnel for fuel
- ❑ cups   (#_____)
- ❑ plates   (#_____)
- ❑ bowls   (#_____)
- ❑ knives   (#_____)
- ❑ forks   (#_____)
- ❑ spoons   (#_____)
- ❑ sharp knife
- ❑ cutting board
- ❑ can opener
- ❑ vegetable peeler
- ❑ large spoon
- ❑ lifter
- ❑ whisk
- ❑ pots   (#_____)
- ❑ fry pan
- ❑ reflector oven
- ❑ outback oven
- ❑ pot lifter
- ❑ fire bar/grate

- ❑ matches
- ❑ lighter
- ❑ fire starter(optional)
- ❑ water filter
- ❑ extra filter
- ❑ water bottle   (#_____)
- ❑ dish pan(s)
- ❑ powder bleach
- ❑ dish soap
- ❑ dish towels   (#_____)
- ❑ dish cloth   (#_____)
- ❑ scratch pad
- ❑ leather work gloves
- ❑ gloves for hot mitts
- ❑ cup-size coffee filter
- ❑ _____
- ❑ _____
- ❑ _____
- ❑ _____

Tricks
- Attach lids to cups with a fishing leader.
- Color code water bottles so everyone has their own color. This way they do not get mixed up.

Clothing Checklist

FAMILY MEMBER:_____

- [ ] underwear   (#_____)
- [ ] t shirts   (#_____)
- [ ] shorts   (#_____)
- [ ] long pants   (#_____)
- [ ] socks   (#_____)
- [ ] long-sleeve shirt   (#_____)
- [ ] warm upper   (#_____)
- [ ] warm lower   (#_____)
- [ ] rain gear
- [ ] bandanas   (#_____)
- [ ] sun hat
- [ ] sunglasses
- [ ] bathing suit
- [ ] towel (small)
- [ ] warm jacket
- [ ] gloves   (#_____)
- [ ] mitts   (#_____)
- [ ] fleece hat
- [ ] fleece socks
- [ ] footwear
- [ ] wet shoes

- [ ] dry shoes
- [ ] hiking boots
- [ ] Gore Tex socks (optional)

- [ ] _____
- [ ] _____

personal items

- [ ] toothpaste
- [ ] toothbrush
- [ ] hair brush
- [ ] medication
- [ ] contact solutions/case
- [ ] glasses

- [ ] _____
- [ ] _____

Tricks

- If two people are close to the same size, bring the extra clothes to fit the larger person. This way the spare clothes will fit two people.
- A pack cloth is a great towel. It will dry quickly and is not nearly as bulky.
- Select quick-drying clothes.

First-Aid / Medical Supplies
··

Trip length: _____ days

Medical information cards for each participant including health
insurance information and emergency phone numbers

BANDAGES / SKIN REPAIR

- ❏ band aids
- ❏ 4x4 gauze pads- sterile
- ❏ 3x3 gauze pads - sterile
- ❏ rolls of gauze 4″
- ❏ steri strips
- ❏ petroleum jelly impregnated
  gauze (for burns)
- ❏ elastic bandage 2″
- ❏ elastic bandage 4″
- ❏ elastic bandage 6″
- ❏ alcohol wipes (optional)

- ❏ mole skin
- ❏ butterfly bandages
- ❏ sanitary napkins (pressure
  bandage)
- ❏ gauze rolls 2″
- ❏ bandage tape
- ❏ waterless hand cleanser
- ❏ iodine soap
- ❏ liquid bandage - new skin
- ❏ petroleum jelly
- ❏ lip balm

MEDICAL SUPPLIES/INFORMATION*

- ❏ thermometer/plastic covers
- ❏ metal finger splint
- ❏ metal mesh splint
- ❏ tweezers
- ❏ sutures
- ❏ first aid booklet

- ❏ epi pens (carried by person
  prescribed to)
- ❏ antibiotic (check with your
  family doctor)
  - _____ dosage-adults
  - _____ dosage-child

---

* For longer wilderness trips, consult your doctor for emergency supplies and recommendations.

OVER-THE-COUNTER MEDICATIONS/REMEDIES

- ❏ anti-nausea tablets
- ❏ motion sickness tablets
- ❏ heartburn/ indigestion tablets
- ❏ sleep-aid tablets
- ❏ muscle relaxant tablets
- ❏ local anesthetic cream
- ❏ anti-diarrhea tablets
- ❏ pain-relief tablets (Ibuprofen)
- ❏ pain and fever reduction tablets (acetaminophen) adult strength
- ❏ pain and fever reduction tablets (acetaminophen) child strength
- ❏ acetaminophen with codeine
- ❏ ASA (not to be given to children)
- ❏ sinus tablets
- ❏ sunburn cream

- ❏ decongestant tablets adult strength
- ❏ decongestant tablets child strength
- ❏ cold tablets daytime
- ❏ cold tablets nighttime
- ❏ cough drops
- ❏ antiseptic throat drops
- ❏ antihistamine tablets
- ❏ allergy medication
- ❏ antibiotic ointment
- ❏ antibiotic ear/eye drops
- ❏ iodine
- ❏ alcohol wipes
- ❏ zinc oxide
- ❏ antiseptic creams

ADDITIONAL SUPPLIES

- ❏ note pad
- ❏ pencil/pen
- ❏ nail clippers

- ❏ lighter/matches
- ❏ scissors
- ❏ safety pins

Tricks

- Bring along some extra zip lock bags, plastic bags, rubber bands and string. They don't take much space and come in handy.
- Make the front of a canoe heavier when paddling into the wind. It's much easier to steer.

Baby Needs

- ❏ Sleepers (#_____)
- ❏ Polar fleece bunting bag
- ❏ cloth diapers (#_____)
- ❏ plastic pants (#_____)
- ❏ diaper pins (#_____)
- ❏ extra pins for hanging clothes
- ❏ disposable diapers (#_____)
- ❏ garbage bag for diapers
- ❏ sun hat
- ❏ warm hat
- ❏ warm mitts
- ❏ rain wear, poncho-style to go over car seat and infant carrier
- ❏ backpack carrier
- ❏ front pack carrier
- ❏ child-size sleeping bag
- ❏ sleeping pad
- ❏ small piece of ensolite
- ❏ rain pants/jacket
- ❏ baby's food
  - _____pablum
  - _____vegetables
  - _____fruit
- ❏ formula

- ❏ plastic bottles and liners
- ❏ infant's snacks
- ❏ baby spoon
- ❏ plastic bowl with snap lid
- ❏ baby toothbrush
- ❏ lightweight car seat (optional)
- ❏ bandana for wipes
- ❏ jumper or swing seat (with secure harnesses)
- ❏ rope for hanging swing / jumper
- ❏ rubber boots
- ❏ winter boots
- ❏ running shoes
- ❏ water shoes
- ❏ mosquito netting for feeding shelter
- ❏ _____
- ❏ _____
- ❏ _____

Tricks

- Bring along a minnow net and identification book to explore pond life.
- Put sticks under packs to keep them dry if you need to paddle in the rain.

Repair Kit

- 5-minute epoxy
- silicone (tube)
- screwdriver (with heads to match equipment)
- duct tape
- sewing supplies: needle, thread, buttons, safety pins
- stitching awl
- spare nuts and screws (to match equipment)
- wire: small pieces for wiring things together
- pliers (small vice grips)
- sandpaper, steel wool
- file
- small container of oil
- sharpening stone for knives
- Swiss Army knife
- extra tips, eyes, split rings etc for fishing equipment

List of items to meet Coast Guard requirements per canoe

1. Sounding signalling device (whistle)

2. Approved PFD for all passengers, appropriate sizes

3. Minimum one paddle per canoe

4. Bailer or manual pump

5. 50 feet of buoyant heaving line

6. Navigation lights if canoe is to be paddled at night

7 Day Menu Planner

	Day 1	Day 2	Day 3
Breakfast			
Morning Snack			
Lunch			
Afternoon Snack			
Dinner			
Bedtime Snack			

Day 4	Day 5	Day 6	Day 7